African Mythology

Enthralling Myths, Fables, and Legends from Africa

© Copyright 2023 - All rights reserved.

The content contained within this book may not be reproduced, duplicated, or transmitted without direct written permission from the author or the publisher.

Under no circumstances will any blame or legal responsibility be held against the publisher, or author, for any damages, reparation, or monetary loss due to the information contained within this book, either directly or indirectly.

Legal Notice:

This book is copyright protected. It is only for personal use. You cannot amend, distribute, sell, use, quote, or paraphrase any part, or the content within this book, without the consent of the author or publisher.

Disclaimer Notice:

Please note the information contained within this document is for educational and entertainment purposes only. All effort has been executed to present accurate, up-to-date, reliable, and complete information. No warranties of any kind are declared or implied. Readers acknowledge that the author is not engaging in the rendering of legal, financial, medical, or professional advice. The content within this book has been derived from various sources. Please consult a licensed professional before attempting any techniques outlined in this book.

By reading this document, the reader agrees that under no circumstances is the author responsible for any losses, direct or indirect, that are incurred as a result of the use of the information contained within this document, including, but not limited to, errors, omissions, or inaccuracies.

Free limited time bonus

Stop for a moment. We have a free bonus set up for you. The problem is this: we forget 90% of everything that we read after 7 days. Crazy fact, right? Here's the solution: we've created a printable, 1-page pdf summary for this book that you're reading now. All you have to do to get your free pdf summary is to go to the following website:

https://livetolearn.lpages.co/enthrallinghistory/

Once you do, it will be intuitive. Enjoy, and thank you!

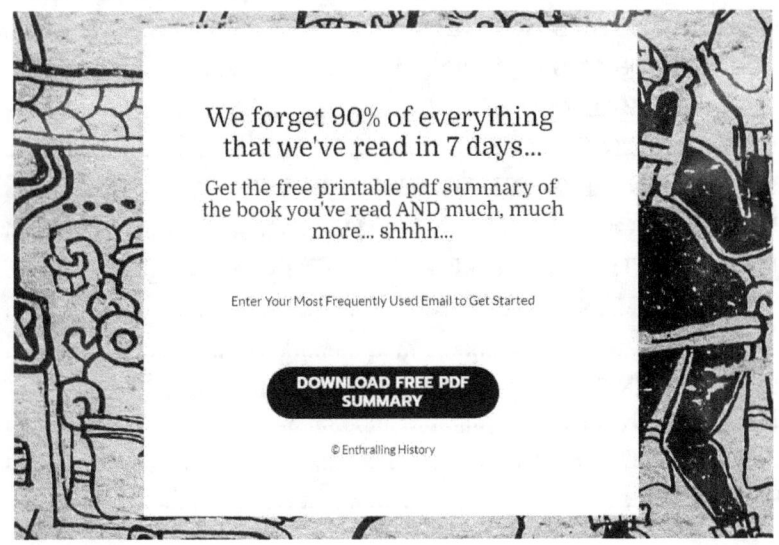

Table of Contents

INTRODUCTION 1
CHAPTER 1: AFRICAN CREATION MYTHS.. 4
CHAPTER 2: GODS AND GODDESSES I... 12
CHAPTER 3: GODS AND GODDESSES II 20
CHAPTER 4: ANIMAL FABLES 26
CHAPTER 5: TRICKSTER TALES... 32
CHAPTER 6: MONSTERS AND MYTHICAL BEASTS............................... 45
CHAPTER 7: HEROES IN AFRICAN MYTH.. 51
CHAPTER 8: MYTHICAL AND LEGENDARY KINGS AND QUEENS 58
CHAPTER 9: SHAMANIC STORIES 70
CONCLUSION 75
HERE'S ANOTHER BOOK BY ENTHRALLING HISTORY THAT YOU MIGHT LIKE.. 77
FREE LIMITED TIME BONUS.. 78
BIBLIOGRAPHY 79

Introduction

Let's begin with two important facts about Africa: Africa is huge, and Africa is very varied. Africa's nearly twelve million square miles of space is enough to fit in the US and China and still have room for half of Europe. (The Mercator map of the globe, which is the one mostly used in atlases, vastly underestimates Africa's true size.)

Africa's landscape is also incredibly varied. There are huge deserts, such as the Kalahari and the Sahara, and there is the long fertile strip called the Nile Valley. There are savannahs, wetlands like the Okavango Delta, and high mountains like Kilimanjaro and the Drakensberg. There are tropical rainforests, rich floodplains, the dramatic landscape of the Rift Valley, and the Great Lakes. African stories reflect this variety of landscape and its creatures, as well as the variety of foods that grow in the different regions, including yams, tubers, bananas, millet, and rice.

Africa also has an immense diversity of people. There are over six thousand different distinct groups speaking two thousand different languages (many people are multilingual, speaking several local languages and French or English too). While we often think of Africa as an untouched continent, unlike, say, Europe or North America, it has been influenced by numerous different cultures over time. There were the Greeks and Romans in Egypt, Islamic cultures from the Middle Ages onward, and Christianity through the Orthodox Coptic and Ethiopian Churches, 19th-century missionaries, and modern Pentecostal evangelists.

Often, traditional stories have been adapted for a new culture or religion, and traditional rites have been reconciled with Christianity or

Islam. For instance, many sangoma healers in South Africa practice Zulu rites but also belong to a church, saying, "God is God, but our ancestors are our ancestors."

Even before the 20th century and the advent of African mega-cities, Africa had developed urban cultures like the Mali Empire, the Benin city-state, and trading cultures in the Sahara and Sahel. In Zanzibar, a cosmopolitan trading culture linked Africa, Arabia, and India. But Khoisan hunter-gatherers, Fulani cattle herders, and Kenyan pastoralists still live in a traditional way, though, in many cases, their lifestyles are threatened by encroaching development and sometimes by climate change.

Though many 19th-century explorers saw Africa as a timeless, eternal continent where nothing ever changed and no civilization had ever been created, Africa has seen numerous great civilizations emerge, starting with ancient Egypt and the Kushite Kingdom of Meroe. Africa was home to the Ethiopian Kingdom of Aksum, the Ghana Empire, the Mali Empire, the Songhai Empire, and the court culture of Ife. Statues and carved heads of great delicacy were made in Ife nearly a thousand years ago; some of them are still displayed on altars, with a festival held in their honor every year. Great Zimbabwe was built by the ancestors of the Shona people in the 9th century and abandoned by 1500; the huge stone Great Enclosure was the center of a city home to some eighteen thousand people.

However, many of these civilizations were not literate. Myths and histories were transmitted orally, with some myths being passed on in the form of performances, such as masked dances. Often, stories and songs were interactive, involving audience participation, and they passed down moral lessons. Proverbs were also immortalized in designs, such as the adinkra textile motifs of Ghana, and through rituals like divination.

Islam brought widespread literacy in Arabic, so stories could be written down, but it also might have changed some of the myths to make them more palatable to a Muslim audience.

Oral tradition was not in any way a free-for-all; the tradition had guardians and keepers, including storytellers, griots (court musicians and poets), and members of sacred societies. In some cases, secret and esoteric aspects of myths were jealously guarded from outsiders; in others, stories were told publicly to underline the importance of a lineage or deity. For instance, Malian griots still sing the Sunjata epic, transmitted through the Kouyate family that goes back to Sunjata Keita's griot, Balla Fasséké, in the early 13th century.

However, rarely has any central authority attempted to create an "authorized version" since so many African myths exist in different forms and are sometimes contradictory. For instance, in one cult, the god Eshu Elegbara is said to be the son of Ogun, the iron god, but this is a minority view. According to another story, he was born to a man called Osunsun and his wife as they were on their way to the market. In yet another story, the enfant terrible Eshu is said to have been born miraculously to the elderly woman Ketu. And yet it's also true that Eshu and Ogun were created by Olorun, the creator. African myths slip, slide, and entangle themselves.

Even when the story is the same, the details may vary. There are more than forty different transcriptions of the Sunjata epic (*African Myths of Origin*), and more versions are continually being created in film or novel form, in children's books and even in books like this one. Spellings often vary, and sometimes, a myth is told by a number of people but with slight changes in names or in the detailed events of the story. This becomes even more confusing with African myths that reached the New World; Nigerian gods turn up in Brazil and Cuba, for instance, but the goddesses show a disconcerting tendency to merge with aspects of the Virgin Mary. Some gods take on the attributes of Christian saints, while river goddesses tend to become sea goddesses. Trickster stories about Anansi and Br'er Rabbit became part of African American and West Indian cultures and, in some cases, were adapted to their new setting.

So, don't expect everything to tie up neatly. African mythology is a fluid universe that continues to evolve to this day. But its roots go way, way back. Let's begin at the beginning with the story of how the world was created.

Chapter 1: African Creation Myths

The simplest of all creation myths is that once upon a time, there was nothing, and then a god created the world so there was something. That is the view of the Banyarwanda of Rwanda.

But other origin myths are more complex. In some cases, creation is a multi-stage process carried out by a number of different deities. Oftentimes, the creation myth not only helps people understand the world but also explains why death exists and why the spiritual and physical realms are no longer the same.

The Senufo of Côte d'Ivoire tell how Kolocolo (Kolotyolo), a god of light and sky, created the world to be inhabited by animals and immortal entities known as the madebele. When the madebele challenged his authority, Kolocolo banished them from the sky and created human beings. These new beings chased the madebele into the bush and took over their farms and houses.

Ever since, diviners have been needed as intermediaries to placate the madebele and use them as messengers to and from the spirit world. The Senufo are exclusively farmers (their blacksmiths, wood carvers, and brass casters live in their villages but belong to other ethnic groups), so the distinction between the village, with its cultivated fields, and the wildness of the bush is crucial to their thinking about the world.

Many creation myths explain why the sky is now so distant. In Sudan, the tale is told of Abradi, the creator who lived in the sky. In the beginning, the sky was close to the earth, and it was easy to come and go between the two. But because the sky was so close, people on Earth had to bend their heads. One woman, who was angry at having to bend over her cooking pots, pushed the sky away with her stirring rod, and Abradi, sulking, moved the sky as far away as he could.

The Nigerian Efik have a similar supreme creator, Abassi. He created the world, and then he made a man and a woman. But he didn't want the man and woman to live on Earth, as he feared competition. When his wife finally convinced him to let them live on Earth, he made two conditions: they must accept the food he gave them, eating with him every night, and they must not have children. However, the woman started tilling the fields to make her own food, and eventually, she and her husband stopped eating with Abassi. They also began to have children. Abassi feared he was forgotten.

Abassi's wife, Atai, who must have felt responsible for his disappointment, wanted to find a way to ensure that he would never ever be forgotten. So, she created death. Men have never forgotten this.

It is intriguing that the Dinka people of Sudan have a myth that combines elements of both of the previous stories. The primordial woman Abuk was only allowed by the supreme creator to plant one grain of millet a day. Feeling rebellious, she decided she would plant more, but she hoed too hard and struck the god with her hoe. The god was so angry that he cut the rope between heaven and Earth.

The Uduk people of Ethiopia have a similar myth in which the creator Arum made the heavens and Earth and linked them together with a huge tree, with its roots in the earth and its branches in heaven. But one day, an old woman cut the tree down. Humans could no longer visit heaven, and death came into the world. (Traditional settlements in Ethiopia and Somalia have trees at their center, and Ethiopian churches are often surrounded by walled forests, so it is perhaps not surprising to find a tree having such an important role.)

Shona mythology tells of Mwari, the creator; he is also called Musikavanhu, "maker of people," Mutangakavara, "he existed at the beginning," or Dzivaguru, "the great water." He filled the world with creatures, and his power can still be seen in the generation of new life and in the blessing of rain. He is both male and female, and he unites other opposites, such as light and darkness and earth and sky. But like so many other creator gods, he is distant. No one can call on Mwari for help without going through the intercession of a spirit medium who is possessed by the ancestors or by other spirits.

Intriguingly, when Christian missionaries translated the Bible into Shona, they used "Mwari" as the word for God.

A much more complex account of creation comes from the Dogon people. There are simple versions, more complex versions, and a rather esoteric version that French anthropologist Marcel Griaule received from a blind hunter and Dogon holy man named Ogotemmeli.

The short version states that Amma created the earth, the sky, and the Nommo spirits before creating other spirits, animals, and people. The earth and sky were separated by a metal post, and they were close together. People did not grow tall, and the hyena put his pawprints on the moon. When the earth and sky quarreled, Amma knocked the post away.

Women were responsible for the separation of the sky from the earth. One day, a woman knocked the sky with her pestle while pounding millet. Amma sent a blacksmith down to the earth on a chain to teach men how to make fire. When Amma was angry and made a drought, the blacksmith pounded on his anvil to make it rain.

Another version tells how the sky god Amma created the Nommo. The Nommo divided himself into four sets of twins. (The Dogon believe twins are magical, as does much of Africa.) One of the twins rebelled against Amma, and another one was sacrificed to atone for the sin. His body was dismembered and scattered throughout the territory, and where pieces of his body fell, there are now shrines.

The ancestors did not die but transformed themselves into snakes. However, Lebe's son became a snake before his father, breaking the natural order. As a consequence, when it was time for Lebe to become a snake, he could not make the change. He died and was buried. When the Dogon decided to migrate, they wanted to dig up Lebe's bones but found a huge snake in the tomb; this snake led them to the Bandiagara escarpment, where they now live.

There is an even more complex version involving primordial incest, three sacred words, and many more stories, which was related to Griaule by Ogotemmeli. This also includes the assertion that the Dogon knew about the invisible star Sirius B, which has been interpreted by author Robert K. G. Temple as evidence that they were in touch with an alien civilization. (Most historians don't find this theory plausible.)

While Griaule was already an expert on Dogon life and religion when he had his series of interviews with Ogotemmeli, basing an analysis of an entire culture on one man's words is like basing the entire history of Christianity on a single text, such as Augustine of Hippo's *Confessions*. Quite a few scholars disagree profoundly with some of Griaule's ideas and even more profoundly with Robert Temple's!

The Dogon people's concern with how death came into the world is echoed by a number of other African myths. One Zulu story tells how the creator decided men should live forever and sent a chameleon to tell them the good news. However, he saw how the humans multiplied and saw them make war on each other, which gave him second thoughts. He called the lizard to him. "I have decided men should die after all," he said. "Go and tell them."

Now, the lizard is fast, and the chameleon is slow, so the lizard got there first. Thus, humans never had a chance; they have always been mortal.

The Bambara of West Africa trace creation to the root sound *Yo*, which was uttered in the void and brought into being the creators: Teliko, Faro, and Pemba. The water spirit Faro created seven heavens, and then she rained to fertilize them. The air spirit Teliko created twins, who were the ancestors of the first humans. And Pemba created the earth, and out of the earth, he made himself a wife, Musokoroni.

However, Musokoroni was a spirit of disorder, and she rebelled against Pemba. Among other evil deeds, she brought death to the world. Eventually, Faro took over from Pemba as ruler of the cosmic balance since Pemba had been unable to maintain it. (Other accounts say that the supreme god sent a flood to cleanse the earth, and Faro rescued humans in her canoe.)

The Maninka creation myth is different, though it shares some aspects with the Bambara account. The creator Mangala created an egg, which contained seeds and two pairs of beings, male and female. Pemba, one of these beings, broke out of the egg and descended to Earth with the seeds, which he planted. However, the earth was impure and sterile because there was no moisture, and he used his own blood to fertilize the earth. The male aspect of the other being was sacrificed, creating water; this was Faro, represented by twin catfish. He brought with him plants, animals, and four pairs of humans. The ancestor of the griots and the ancestor of the blacksmiths then descended separately from heaven, and finally, Pemba's female twin, Muso Koroni, joined Pemba.

Pemba continued to be rebellious and destructive, even more so after Muso Koroni arrived. Eventually, Faro had to deal with him. The Niger River shows the track he took toward Pemba's hideout in the delta.

Far more charming is the Kono creation story from Sierra Leone. There was no light in the world until Sa gave birds the ability to sing. The sound of birdsong brought light to the world.

The Jewish creation story doesn't give God any motivation for creation. God just creates. But African creator gods are often motivated by boredom. The Bambuti pygmies say that Khvum (Khonvoum) the creator was bored of being alone. There was no one to make or share his food, so he filled his bag with nkula nuts and made them into people.

The Bunyoro, who live near Lake Victoria, also see boredom as the motivation for creation, though this time, there are two primordial beings involved. They tell how, at the beginning, there were two brothers, Ruhanga and Nkya. Nkya was bored, so Ruhanga separated the earth from the heavens and made the sun. Earth and heaven remained close together, with Nkya living on Earth and Ruhanga in heaven. Nkya got burned, so Ruhanga made clouds to cover the sun and then made the moon so there was light in the darkness. Nkya wanted shade, so Ruhanga made trees and threw water down from heaven as rain. But Nkya complained that the rain was cold, so Ruhanga made him a shelter and showed him how to use tools.

Nkya had four sons. The oldest was Kantu. The others were nameless, so Nkya sent them to Ruhanga to get names. Ruhanga set them tests and then named the boys Servant, Herdsman, and King. However, Kantu was angry that Ruhanga did not give him the kingship, so the sons had a falling-out with each other. Nkya, fed up with life on Earth, returned to live with Ruhanga and knocked away the supports that kept heaven and Earth together.

The Yoruba have several different explanations of creation. First, there is a story that tells how Orisa-nla the creator lived with his slave Atunda in a formless void. But one day, Atunda, fed up with playing second fiddle, rebelled against his master. He rolled a huge boulder down a hill. The god shattered into a myriad of fragments, each one becoming a separate god or orisha.

Then, there is the story of how Olodumare the supreme being asked Orisa-nla to make a world out of magic earth. Oris-nla did so, but it was Olodumare who breathed the soul into each animal and human to complete creation.

Or there is the story of how Olorun (Supreme God) chose Oduduwa as his assistant, giving him a cockerel (a young rooster), a handful of soil, and a palm nut. Oduduwa came down from heaven on a chain and found a mass of water. He threw the soil down to create the earth and then set down the cockerel, which scratched at the earth to create rivers, seas, hills, and valleys. After this, Oduduwa planted the palm nut, which grew into a sixteen-branched tree, with each branch representing a Yoruba kingdom.

Creation didn't go too well, though. According to one story, Eshu Elegbara was jealous. He had thought Olorun would pick him to help create the world and was upset that Oduduwa had been chosen instead. So, he got his rival too drunk to do the work properly.

There's also an interesting Yoruba story that suggests women have a much bigger part in creation than the Judeo-Christian canon. Seventeen odu (gods) came down to Earth, and they worked to prepare a sacred grove for each of them. However, they left Osun out. She sat quietly by, plaiting her hair with a comb. Because they left her out, nothing they did was successful, so they returned to heaven and complained to Olodumare about their lack of success. Olodumare, counting them, found only sixteen odu. "What happened to Osun?" he asked and told them they needed to recognize her.

In another story, the supreme god doesn't actually mean to create anything; instead, he vomits the universe into creation. The Kuba people in Congo say that the god Mboom (also known as Bumba or Mbombo) was in darkness and vomited up the sun, moon, stars, animals, birds, fish, and humans. These animals, in turn, vomited up others. The crocodile vomited snakes, the goat vomited horned animals, one man vomited up ants, and another vomited up plants.

Even this story comes in different versions. Some say that Mboom initially worked with the god Ngaan, but they quarreled. Ngaan then created water creatures and harmful creatures, such as crocodiles and snakes. And there are later episodes in which Mboom's nine sons, each called Woot, create the arts and crafts and human knowledge. For instance, one forges iron.

Look back to ancient Egypt, and you will find several different accounts of creation. Different myths seem to have developed or gained prominence over time as different gods were adopted by the ruling dynasties. Local cults also had different myths, which had to be reconciled (or not) once Egypt became unified.

In Heliopolis, for instance, the sun god, Atum, spat (or, according to other accounts, masturbated) into the water, which created Shu and Tefnut (air and water). Their children were Geb and Nut (earth and sky), and their children were Osiris, Isis, Set, and Nephthys. These eight gods, together with Atum, made the Ennead or Great Nine.

But in Hermopolis, it was the Ogdoad—eight gods, or rather four pairs of male and female deities. The gods had frog heads, and the goddesses had serpent heads. The Ogdoad inhabited the primeval waters. The union of the Ogdoad created the mound from which the sun, Ra, emerged to light the world. The Ogdoad resemble other African multiples like the Nommo and the Woot, and like them, the Ogdoad are not distinguished in any way, though this hasn't stopped scholars from trying to give them different functions.

In Thebes (today's Luxor), it was Amun who created the universe. His call broke the silence, and at his cry, the primeval mound arose, along with the Ogdoad and the pantheon of the gods. (The priesthood of Amun neatly took over the tradition of Hermopolis but set its god neatly on top.)

In Memphis, Ptah was the creator god. He was said to have "crafted the design of the world in his heart," according to one hymn, and brought the world into being through speaking it aloud.

Then, there is the story of how the sun god Ra existed alone in a watery void. The Benben mound (later seen as a pyramid) emerged, with a lotus flower out of which Ra stepped. He then created the deities of air (god Shu) and water (goddess Tefnut) by union with his own shadow. He created life by uttering the secret name of every plant and animal. Humans were created from his tears and sweat.

The Atum and Ra myths were reconciled with that of Ptah through the idea that Ptah had created Atum and Ra through his original thought. This seems typical of other African myths since there are different levels of the creator, with a more distant original creator god who delegates much of the specific work of creation to junior gods.

By the way, Atum is also the god of endings. In the Coffin Texts of the First Intermediate Period, quite early in Egyptian history, he tells Osiris that after a million years, the universe will revert to the state of the primordial waters. Only he and Osiris of all the gods will remain, doing so in the form of water snakes.

In all of these myths, the original state of being is the primeval water. That seems appropriate for Egypt, a land whose very existence was based on the Nile flooding. But which of these stories is the *right* one? Egyptians don't seem to have been overly bothered; their stories were as fluid as the Nile itself.

But then, many African myths accept that there is more than one way of explaining creation. For instance, the Fang people in Cameroon say that the first being, Mebege, created the world, but they also say that the world was created by a spider that came from heaven on its own spiderweb. That may not make sense to you, but it does to them.

Chapter 2: Gods and Goddesses I

Africa has a wide range of gods and goddesses, and that's been the case for the last five millennia, at least. The first gods we can definitely identify in Africa are those of ancient Egypt. There are more than 1,500 of them, some widely worshiped and others restricted to a single locality. They often (though not always) have animal heads on human bodies. They're also often presented in the form of a definitive set of myths, but Egyptian mythology actually developed over time, and different localities had different versions. Upper and Lower Egypt, which were originally separate kingdoms, often had separate deities or gods with different emphases or different attributes.

Some gods were identified with a particular location, like Montu at Thebes, Sobet the crocodile god at Kom Ombo (where there is an impressive collection of mummified crocodiles in the temple museum) and at Faiyum, and Khnum the ram-headed god at Elephantine. (Montu was eventually demoted by Amun as the main god at Thebes, being described as the son of Amun and the goddess Mut.)

The earliest well-attested Egyptian god is Ra or Re, the sun god. He is found in inscriptions of the Old Kingdom by the Fifth Dynasty after the pyramids of Giza were built. Ra is often shown as a falcon carrying the sun disk on his head or is depicted just as a sun disk. He is said to have been the first pharaoh of Egypt.

As the sun god, Ra carries the sun on his solar barque (ship) during its daily journey through the sky and then over the horizon (akhet) into the underworld (Duat) at sunset. He emerges again at dawn after a night of struggling with Apep, the underworld snake.

Later, Ra was merged with other gods, with there being gods like Amun-Ra, Ra-Atum, and Ra-Horakhty (merged with Horus, another falcon-headed god). He was given Khepri (scarab) and Khnum (ram) as his morning and night manifestations.

Amun was a creator god and the patron god of Thebes. His cult came to prominence in the New Kingdom with the Eighteenth Dynasty, which based its capital in Thebes and vastly extended Amun's temple in Karnak. Amun is shown with blue skin and is associated with the air. He is transcendental and self-created. His name means "hidden" or "invisible." His titles included lord of truth, father of the gods, maker of men, creator of all animals, lord of things that are, and creator of the staff of life.

Ptah is shown as a mummified man with a green face, and he is part of the triad of Memphis, together with his wife, the lion-headed Sekhmet, and their son, Nefertem.[1] Ptah, as creator, incubates the idea of the world and is able to manifest it by speaking it forth, which makes him a god revered by craftsmen. He is actually quite a good father for an architect since he symbolizes the transformation of mental plans into physical reality.

Later on in the history of Egypt, the god Osiris became important, alongside his wife Isis and son Horus. Osiris is specifically a pharaonic god; the pharaoh becomes Osiris when he dies, and many mortuary temples of pharaohs include statues of the pharaoh-as-Osiris, for instance at Abu Simbel. Originally, Osiris was worshiped at Abydos, which was a major royal necropolis very early in Egyptian history, along with Anubis, the jackal-headed god.

Osiris is the god of death, taking the title "Lord of Silence" (that is, of the underworld), but he is also a god of fertility. His green skin symbolizes putrefaction and the green of growth. He is shown with the false beard of a pharaoh and with crossed arms, holding a crook and a flail.

---

[1] The sage Imhotep, who designed Djoser's magnificent step pyramid and funerary complex, was eventually made into a god. Since he came from Memphis, the idea eventually arose that he was another son of Ptah.

Osiris's story is one of death and resurrection. He was murdered by his evil brother Set (or Seth), who cut him into pieces and then scattered the pieces all over Egypt. This, according to Egyptian thinking, would have stopped Osiris from being able to go to the afterlife. However, Osiris's wife, Isis, traveled around Egypt to find the pieces of his body. She was able to revive the corpse and became pregnant, giving birth to Horus.

Little figures of Osiris were filled with dirt and then planted with wheat and watered. One of these was found in the tomb of Tutankhamun. These figures symbolized new life.

Isis, Osiris's wife, was the mother of both Horus and the pharaoh. Pharaoh Seti I is even shown being breastfed by Isis in his temple at Abydos, and other pharaohs showed themselves in this way as well. Isis wears a throne on her head and is, in a way, a personification of the throne, a symbol of the power of kingship.

During the Ptolemaic period and under the Romans, Isis's cult became popular outside Egypt, as she was seen as one of the most important mother goddesses. In one hymn of this period, she is described as the creator "through what her heart conceived and her hands created."[2]

Set, Osiris's brother, was the god of storms, deserts, and disorder. Egypt divided itself into the Black Land and the Red Land—fertile land and desert. Set was the lord of the Red Land. However, he also had a positive role, as he accompanied Ra's barque during the night to protect him against the snake Apep. Set was the father of Anubis, the underworld judge. Few reliefs show Set, but when he does appear, he is shown in black with an animal head with flat-topped ears and a forked tail.

Horus avenged his father, Osiris, and expelled Set from Egypt, becoming pharaoh. Shown as a falcon or as a falcon-headed man, Horus was a sky god associated with kingship and healing. His temple in Edfu had a roof terrace for sky rituals and narrow staircases up which the golden idol of the god would be taken to "recharge."

The ruling pharaoh was seen as a manifestation of Horus, with one of his official names being known as the "Horus name." In some early

---

[2] Žabkar, Louis V. Hymns to Isis in Her Temple at Philae. Brandeis University Press. 1988.

accounts, Horus is mentioned as the son and helper of Ra. Other inscriptions say he was the son of Nut and Geb (the earth and sky), which would make him the brother rather than the son of Isis and Osiris. However, by the Ptolemaic period, the Osiris version had become definitive.

Horus was tasked by Isis with protecting the people of Egypt against Set, who was ejected from the Egyptian throne. In other words, he was tasked with protecting the fertile land and the civilized order against the barren desert and nomadic barbarians. It's likely that the story of this struggle represents early power struggles between different smaller kingdoms. Horus is often associated with Lower Egypt (the Nile Delta and Cairo), while Set is associated with Upper Egypt (the rest of the Nile Valley).

These were the major Egyptian gods; there were many others, but they were typically seen as less important. Thoth, shown most commonly with the head of an ibis but sometimes with the head of a baboon, was the son of Set. He was the god of the moon, wisdom, scribes, and the written word. Together with his wife Ma'at, he stands on Ra's solar barque. Thoth was seen as a magician and the judge of the dead. In many ways, Thoth represented balance, and Ma'at represented truth, order, and law. In fact, the word Ma'at means measure or order.

Ma'at is often seen as a tiny figure accompanying a king or as a hieroglyph. She wears a single feather in her headband. Her task was to regulate the constellations in the sky and the seasons on Earth. Her feather was important because it was the weight that was used to balance the scales in the Duat when the souls of the dead were to be weighed. Kings often used her name as part of their regal name. For instance, Ramesses II took the name Usermaatre Setepenre (the Ma'at of Ra is powerful, chosen of Ra), while his father Seti I took the name Menmaatre (the Ma'at of Ra is established).

Ma'at was the first deity that Ra created. It was the king's task to maintain Ma'at (justice or, more generally, order) in the double kingdoms of Egypt. So, though she doesn't get much notice in most books of Egyptian mythology, Ma'at was actually a very important god.

Anubis, the jackal-headed god of the underworld, is always black, which was an auspicious color in Egypt and symbolic of regeneration, like the fertile soil of the Nile Valley. In the Old Kingdom, Anubis was the most important god of the dead, but eventually, Osiris became more important. Anubis became the patron of mummification and a psychopomp (one who leads the dead soul to the underworld). When Set turned himself into an angry leopard to attack Osiris, Anubis took a hot iron rod and branded Set's skin; that is how the leopard got his spots and is also why priests who celebrated funerary rites wore leopard skins.

Hathor was an important goddess. She was sometimes shown as a cow and sometimes as a woman with cow ears, cow horns, and a sun disk. She was the goddess of the sun, sexuality, and music. The jingling sistrum was used in her worship. (It's also intriguingly used in the worship of the Ethiopian Church.)

Hathor is known as the Eye of Ra and is the divine counterpart of the queen (or Great Wife, to give her the Egyptian title). She was said to be the consort of Ra and the mother (or consort) of Horus. As the Eye of Ra, she had a wrathful aspect, carrying out Ra's commands.

In one story, Ra sends Hathor to punish humans for rebelling against him. In her anger, she turns into the lioness-headed goddess Sekhmet and massacres thousands of people. When Ra sees this, he decides to save the rest of humanity. He does this by dyeing beer red so that it looks like blood. The bloodthirsty Sekhmet drinks the "blood," becomes drunk, and passes out. As she sleeps, she turns into the peaceful Hathor again.

Khnum, a ram-headed god, was associated with water and procreation. He was said to mold human children out of the Nile's silt and place the tiny babies in their mothers' wombs. He was worshiped on the island of Elephantine (Aswan) together with his consort, Satis, and his daughter, Anuket. Khnum was the guardian of the source of the Nile.

Taweret was a very popular goddess, though she did not have a high status. She was the hippopotamus goddess and the protector of women in childbirth. (That's logical, as hippos are very protective mothers.) Many Taweret amulets have been found; these would have given many women confidence as their due date approached.

Finally, Aten was originally an attribute of Ra, the sun disk he bore on his head. However, under Akhenaten and his immediate successors, Aten was made into a transcendent god. He was already being worshiped under Amenhotep III, but Akhenaten made his worship obligatory and exclusive. Aten's temples, unlike the dim sanctuaries of other gods, were in the open air, and Aten was shown not as a human but as a simple disk, sometimes extending multiple rays ending in hands as a sign of blessing. Whether the abstraction of this god was too much for the Egyptians or whether Akhenaten's family lost a power struggle against the priesthood of Amun, Aten didn't last. The regular gods were soon reinstated after Akhenaten's death.

Nubia, farther south of the Nile Valley, was, at times, part of Egypt. At one point, Nubia actually provided Egypt with a dynasty of pharaohs (the Kushite or Black Pharaohs). It's not surprising that the Nubian religion was largely influenced by the Egyptians, with the two religions sharing many of the same gods. For instance, Amun was worshiped at the Kushite capital of Napata, and Mut (a mother goddess) was particularly popular.

There were also a number of specifically Nubian gods. Dedwen, or Dedun, was the god of the four directions and also the god of incense. Under the Kushites, he became aggregated with Osiris. The lion-headed Apedemak was particularly popular in the Meroitic period (300 BCE–350 CE) when the Nubians tried to get rid of Egyptian influences in their culture. He was the god of war and kingship.

In the Horn of Africa, Aksum in Ethiopia is now a major site of the Ethiopian Church, but before the 4th-century conversion to Christianity, Aksum had its own religion. There's only fragmentary information available, but it appears the religion of this early empire was originally a Semitic religion similar to the pagan religions of southern Arabia. The original triad of the sun, moon, and Venus was slightly altered in Aksum and became sea, earth, and Venus (Behr, Medr, and Ashtar) instead. There was also a war god named Mahram, who was specifically the protector of the Aksumite ruler. So, in a way, Aksumite myths were not "African" but Middle Eastern. (Later, Arabia would have a much more profound influence on Africa through the spread of Islam.)

The Berbers or, to give them their proper name, the Imazighen nowadays are mostly Muslim, but archaeology has found traces of their original beliefs. Ancestor worship was a key part of their religion. Often, they went to sleep overnight in tombs, where they believed they would have dreams that divined the future.[3]

---

[3] Their use of tombs as worship centers may have left its mark on the cult of marabouts, Muslim saints, whose tombs are often visited by the faithful and which is specific to North and West Africa.

The Greek historian Herodotus mentions the Berbers worshiping the sun and moon, and Saint Augustine of Hippo says they worshiped rocks. They seem to have been eclectic and even magpie people, taking gods from Egypt and later from Greece and Rome.

The Akan religion of the Ashanti people in Ghana is still practiced by some Ghanaians, though the country is largely Christian. Many people blend some aspects of the Akan religion and thought with a professed Christian belief.

The Ashanti believe that the supreme god, Nyame, created the world but is no longer involved with it. He has two other names—Onyankopon Kwame and Odomankoma—and has sometimes been confused with the Christian Trinity. However, he is a single god with three aspects, not three interlinked godheads.

Nyame's consort is the earth mother Asase Yaa or Afua. She is the earth mother and the mother of the dead, so she has two different aspects, one as an old woman and the other as a beautiful young woman. Asase Yaa is worshiped in the open fields, not in temples.

There are various stories of why Nyame withdrew from the earth. One says that he was annoyed by someone pounding yam and climbed back into heaven. Asase Yaa tried to reach him by making a tower of mortars, but the tower collapsed. Nyame and his wife have been separated ever since, as has the earth and heaven.

Of more direct importance in the Akan religion are the abosom, the lower deities, which are similar to the Vodou lwa (loa or loi) or to the orishas in the Yoruba religion. These include the river god Tano, the thunder god Bobowissi, and the bush god Bia. Anansi the spider is another of the lower gods.

Below the gods are the various spirits. There are tree spirits, animal spirits, and spirits that animate amulets. Below these but of still great importance to individuals are the ancestor spirits, Nsamanfo. They are venerated, often by having libations poured on their graves, and can be a source of advice or assistance but only to their own lineage (except in the case of former kings, whose entire kingdom is their "family").

The Dogon recognize Amma, the sky god, but he is distant from them. More relevant to daily life are the primordial spirits known as Nommo and Lebe, the first ancestor and the first man to die. Lebe, as a huge snake, led the Dogon to their home on the Bandiagara escarpment. They are worshiped through sacrifices.

Some gods are dual in nature. The Efik refer to Abassi Onyong (the god above) and Abassi Isiong (the god below), and the Lugbara people in Uganda, Sudan, and Congo have two similar gods: Adroa and Adro. Adroa is the transcendent sky god, while Adro is an earth god and, as the "bad Adro," is associated with death. Bad Adro's children are spirits who follow people at night; you must never look backward when you are walking at night, or they will kill you.

The fact that the supreme god is so distant from the world makes it necessary to have diviners or priests who can bridge the gap through sacrifices or through visions and trances. The Turkana in Kenya believe that contact between Akuj and the people can only be made through a diviner called an emuron. All diviners come from the same clan, though the office isn't hereditary. Akuj is the provider of rain and has a dual aspect since he is both a benevolent god who brings rain to fertilize crops and a dangerous god who brings thunder, lightning, and floods.

Chapter 3: Gods and Goddesses II

One of the most complex and developed pantheons in African mythology is the orisha pantheon of the Yoruba people. Many of its gods are also well known outside of Africa since, along with the Akan gods, knowledge of them crossed the Atlantic with slaves. They are known in New World spiritual paths like Candomblé and Voodoo (or Vodou). In some ways, the Yoruba pantheon fills in the missing link between the distant creator god and the subsidiary deities who concern themselves with life on earth, making it a theologically complex creation.

It is also a fluid pantheon. Some gods have different names in different areas of Yorubaland, as well as new names in the Americas. Some gods even cross genders; in some traditions, the goddess Olokun is male. Different religious societies tell different stories about the gods and give gods different tasks. So, it's difficult to condense the Yoruba pantheon into a rigid structure. Nonetheless, although the details differ, the overall shape of the pantheon is the same, whoever's telling the story.

Olorun or Olodumare is the creator god and prime mover who infused the world with *ase*, or life force. Like other creator gods, he has withdrawn from the world. His offspring, Orisa-nla, is the Maker who created the physical part of the world for Olodumare to give life to.

Orunmila, the god of fate, was present at the creation and knows everything that is and will come to be. He is the god of wisdom and is in charge of divination. Osanyin is the god of herbal medicines and healing, and Ogun is the god of iron, steel, and war. Oaths are taken on a machete in Ogun's name, and he is the patron of hunters, blacksmiths, warriors, and ironworkers. Nowadays, he has become the god of taxi drivers and truckers.

Shango is a wrathful and energetic god who creates thunder and lightning. He is also a royal ancestor of the Yoruba and the most feared of the Yoruba gods, which is why he is always called on at the coronation of Yoruba kings. While Lady Oshun was married to Orunmila and shared the patronage of divination with him, she fell in love with Shango at a drum festival and became his third and most favored wife.

An important god is Eshu, who is a mediator between the creator Olodumare and his world. He reports to Olodumare on what is happening on Earth and checks that the right sacrifices are being made. He always has a place in a Yoruba shrine, no matter which god it is devoted to. Eshu is also a trickster, though he usually has a reason for his tricks. For instance, his tricks show people that the way they are behaving is not right.

Oshun is the river goddess and a seductive woman who is wealthy and generous. She is given bracelets and ornaments of brass in Nigeria, where it once was an expensive, imported metal. In the Americas, where brass is not so valuable, she is given gold. Her color is yellow. Oshun represents the healing powers of coolness and water and is worshiped in a sacred grove on the banks of her river. She is also the goddess of love and pleasure.

Oshun is sometimes disruptive. She once refused to make sacrifices, so Eshu sold her three dolls filled with magic that made them dance. She gave him all the brass she had to buy the dolls, but when she got home, she found that Eshu had taken the magic away. The dolls were nothing more than wood. Somehow, money never stays long with Oshun, but she always manages to get more; just like the river, she is always flowing.

She is also sometimes imprudent, to say the least. In the city of Oro, Oshun had so many children that there was no room in her house for her to sit down. However, she is willing to go to great lengths to defend her people. When the city of Ido was besieged by enemies and the people were taken away as slaves, Oshun rescued her people. They didn't know their way back to Ido, so Oshun turned herself into a river and flowed back to Ido, carrying the people along in the water.

Yemoja is another water goddess, the deity of the Ogun River. She is also the patron of pregnant women. While Oshun is flirtatious and sexy, Yemoja is a mother. Her name means "mother of fish children," and she is the mother of all the orishas. She is sometimes shown as a mermaid, though in Nigeria, she is strictly a river goddess and yields the sea to the god Olokun. In Cuba and Brazil, on the other hand, Yemoja has become the sea goddess. Her color in Yorubaland is usually white; in the Caribbean and the Americas, it is light blue.

There are over a thousand divinities in the Yoruba pantheon. Some accounts put the number as high as six thousand. Some of these gods are local, such as the goddesses of the different rivers; there is Oya (the Niger River), Yemoja (the Ogun River), and Otin. Some are deified humans; these might be rulers of city-states or people who did great things, such as Moremi, the woman who saved the city of Ife. No disrespect is meant to any gods who have been missed, but space is limited!

The Igbo, who live around the Niger River in southern Nigeria, espouse the Odinala religion. Chukwu is their supreme creator god, but as is often the case in African religions, he is seen as a distant god who doesn't occupy himself much with the affairs of the world. His daughter, Ala, is an earth goddess and fertility goddess. She is also the ruler of the underworld and the mother and queen of the ancestors. This combination of fertility and underworld roles is not unusual in African mythology and is another way in which many African goddesses (and some gods, such as Osiris) have dual aspects.

Gods can be dangerous. Ala is usually benevolent, but she can turn violent if she is offended. She maintains justice and morality and can inflict serious punishment. Her particular emblem is the royal python, which is greatly respected by the Igbo. Pythons are allowed to wander wherever they like, including in the villages and even into houses. If one is killed by accident, it is given a proper funeral.

Naturalist J. A. Skertchly, in his account of his travels in Dahomey, tells of the "fetish house" where the royal pythons lived. Should anyone kill a python, even by accident, he would be placed in a hut that was then set on fire. If the man tried to save himself by running from the flames, the women who guarded the shrine would club him to death. Anyone meeting a python in the street had to worship it by pouring palm wine on the ground, and if a python crawled up to a baby, the child would be given to the snake as its new priest and brought up in the temple. The pythons, in short, ran the place.

The agbara or arusi are lesser spirits that represent natural forces. Amadioha is sometimes shown as Ala's consort and is the god of thunder and lightning. Like Ala, he is a god who visits justice on malefactors, either with lightning bolts or by sending a swarm of bees after them. His color is red, and he is often shown as a light-skinned man of high rank. He brings wealth to his personal devotees and is often prayed to for redress, for help against infertility, and for material betterment.

Ikenga is a horned god, and a statue of him is found in many Igbo households. The image of Ikenga represents the power to achieve success. While an American might read self-help books to get by in the world, an Igbo will make sacrifices to his (and sometimes her) Ikenga.[4] Ikenga is also the patron of blacksmiths and industry.

However, Ikenga doesn't always get respect. The relationship between gods and humans is different from the submission to God that is expected in the Abrahamic religions. Ikenga has to work for his keep; otherwise, people are likely to say, "If the Ikenga's not working, just chop him up for firewood!"

Njoko Ji is the god of yams. This is not an unimportant task, as the yam is one of the main foods in Igboland, and the New Yam Festival is one of the major events of the year. While most Igbo nowadays are Christians, Igbo festivals like the New Yam Festival (Iri ji) and masked dances are still performed. Sometimes, they are treated as "traditions" rather than religion to reconcile them with the Christian faith.

A great empire to the west of Yorubaland was that of Dahomey (now in modern Benin), inhabited by the Fon people. The Fon pantheon, or Vodun, has certain similarities to the Yoruba gods, but it is organized in a more complex way, with several different pantheons under the supreme god Nana Buluku, who is both male and female.

The sky pantheon is headed by the twin god Mawu-Lisa, the creator of the material world. Mawu is female and represents the earth, the west, the moon, and the night. Her time is sunrise. She is gentle, forgiving, nurturing, and fertile. Lisa is male and represents the sky, the east, the sun, and the day. His time is sunset, and he can be strong and ruthless.

---

[4] While Ikenga is mostly found in men's shrines, women who have high status may also have an Ikenga.

Mawu-Lisa's son Agè is the god of the wilderness, the forest, and the hunt.

Gu is another sky pantheon god. He is the fifth son of Mawu-Lisa. He is the god of iron, weapons, tools, craft, and war; this is a potent combination in West Africa, where the Edo Kingdom of Benin, the Yoruba Kingdom of Oyo, and the Fon Kingdom of Dahomey all came to power between 1400 and 1700 through aggressive conquests. All three cultures share a similar iron and weapons god (Ogun in the Yoruba and Edo cultures), showing how central the smelting of iron was to weaponry and to the expansion of these states.[5]

The thunder and sea pantheons are headed by Sogbo, or Hevioso, an androgynous sky-dwelling god. Sogbo gave birth to all the other gods of the thunder pantheon and sent them to live in the sea, which was ruled by Agbè and his twin wife, Naètè. The sea gods control storms and rain, and the youngest of them, Gbade, is a trickster who enjoys making the noise of thunder.

Then, there is the earth pantheon, headed by Sagbata, a son of Mawu-Lisa. Sagbata took as much as he could of the sky's riches to Earth, but he could not take the rain, which Sogbo kept under his control. That is why Earth doesn't always get the rain it needs, as the two gods don't always get on well with each other.

However, Legba, Mawu-Lisa's youngest son, found out from Sagbata that there was a drought on Earth. He sent a little bird (Wututu) to tell Sagbata to make a huge fire. Meanwhile, he told Mawu-Lisa that Earth was burning up and would burn heaven too if he didn't stop it. Mawu-Lisa told Sogbo to let all his stored-up rain fall as quickly as possible. Ever since then, Wututu has lived on Earth and can be sent as a messenger to Mawu-Lisa if there isn't enough rain.

Legba is an unpredictable trickster god. Though in the previous story he seems to act benevolently, it's also said that he was responsible for the drought because he'd previously told Sogbo to stock up on rain. Because of his unpredictability, he's one of the gods who is always propitiated by the Fon just to keep him on their side.

---

[5] Barnes, Sandra T & Ben-Amos, Paula. "Benin, Oyo, and Dahomey: Warfare, State Building, and the Sacralization of Iron in West African History." *Expedition Magazine* 25.2 (1983). Penn Museum, 1983.

The Maasai, the cattle-herding nomads of Kenya, have a rather different view of things compared to the complex West African pantheons. That might reflect the fact that their world is rather less complex than the city-states, trading entrepots, and empires of the West. They have just two gods: the supreme god En-kai and his wife Olapa, who represent the sun and moon. Some say that En-Kai is an androgynous god.

En-kai made the first man, Naiteru-kop, and gave him the earth to live on. One night, En-kai told all the people to leave their kraals (compounds) open. Some did, but some didn't. Those who did found cattle in their compounds in the morning, and they became the Maasai. The others had no cattle and became the ancestors of other peoples. But it may not surprise you to know that there are other versions of the story of how the Maasai got their cattle. There will actually be another one in the next chapter!

Chapter 4: Animal Fables

Examine earlier books of African folk tales, and you will find many of them full of stories about animals. That doesn't mean that animal stories are a huge part of African mythology and folklore; it probably has more to do with the fact that early European collectors found them easier to sympathize with and understand than historical tales or myths of African gods and heroes. Tales about humans make assumptions about social norms, many of which, like polygamy, the prevalence of half-sibling relationships, veneration of ancestors, and initiation ceremonies, were antipathetic to early Africanists and differed widely from Western society.

The animals in African stories were often interesting to Europeans because they were distinctively African animals. Early Africans in the area inhabited by the Khoisan (Bushmen) painted elands (spiral-horned antelopes) and praying mantises on rocks thirty thousand years ago, and San/Khoisan mythology still centers on these creatures. Khaggen, the praying mantis, is a shape-changing trickster with a rock hyrax (a rabbit-like animal) wife and an adopted porcupine daughter. The eland, on the other hand, is a power animal that can help a San shaman go into trance.

Power animals were often "master animals," the main food animal of a people. For instance, the buffalo was the master animal of the South African Baronga, who believed they had a special pact or covenant with the buffalo. Breaking that pact brought dire consequences.

Some animals were teachers. The Greeks had Aesop's fables, in which animal stories were used to make a moral point. For instance, Aesop praises the ant for its industrious nature. But the Berber and Kabyle story tells how an ant taught men how to farm. A man and a woman saw an ant trying to remove the husk of a grain of wheat and learned from it how to thresh wheat, how to make flour, how to cook it, and how to sow it. They sowed it at the wrong time of the year, though, and the seeds failed to sprout, so the ant had to come back and tell them the right season for sowing.

Sometimes, animals had knowledge that men wanted but weren't willing to teach them. According to the Bambuti (Pygmies) of the central African forests, chimpanzees were once human but fell out with the others and withdrew to the forest. This wouldn't have mattered except for the fact that only the chimpanzees had the secret of fire. A Bambuti decided to make friends with the chimpanzees and visited them often. The chimpanzees would give him bananas and let him warm himself by the fire, something that he very much appreciated. However, they never volunteered to show him how to make fire.

The Bambuti thought up a plan to steal the fire. One day, he turned up to the chimpanzees' village wearing a long fake tail. He sat down as normal to eat some bananas and chat, but as he sat by the fire, his tail—made out of pounded tree bark—began to burn. He jumped up and down in pain as if the tail was real. "Help! Help!" he cried. The chimpanzees thought that was the funniest thing they'd seen in a while, and they were so helpless with laughter that they didn't notice when he began to run. He got all the way back to his village before the chimpanzees understood what he'd done. He had stolen the secret of fire, and the Bambuti have had it ever since.

Snakes are often important in African stories, like the Igbo's Royal Python. The Lunda people believed the python Chinawezi governed the earth and all bodies of water, including rivers, streams, pools, and watering holes. The Woyo of the Lower Congo see Bunzi, the snake daughter of the Great Mother Mboze, as the rainbow (which does look like a snake) and rainmaker.

A Fulani story from the Sahel tells how a woman had twins. One was a boy, and one was a snake that had ninety-four scales, each the color of a different type of cattle. The boy was called Ilo. She didn't give the snake a name, but she hid him under a pot.[6] When she died many years later, Ilo built his brother a hut to live in and brought him milk every morning for his breakfast. Ilo looked after their cattle. The brothers became wealthy, and they had a big herd.

The snake told Ilo that he must never marry a small-breasted woman because if such a woman ever saw the snake, he would have to leave. Of course, Ilo fell in love with a small-breasted woman, but he didn't forget what his snake brother had said. He built a big wall around the snake's hut. No one could see over it, and the snake was happy and secure.

But one day, curiosity got the better of Ilo's wife. She took a big pot and used it to stand on to look over the wall. There, she saw the huge snake lying on the ground, soaking up the sun.

The snake slithered down to the river, followed by all the cattle from his brother's compound. He explained to Ilo what had happened and said that he had to go and that the cattle would follow him. However, he would share fairly with his brother; Ilo could keep as many cattle as he could touch with a stick. The rest would follow the snake into the water.

Ilo cut himself a stick from a blackwood tree that stood nearby and touched as many cattle as he could before the herd disappeared into the river. And that is why Fulani herdsmen always use a walking stick made from blackwood.

A snake also figures in the alternative story of how the Maasai got their cattle. In the beginning, the Maasai had no cattle. The Dorobo (non-Maasai people) possessed them all. A Dorobo man lived with a snake and an elephant and its calf. One day, the Dorobo found a cow. The snake sneezed and gave the man a rash, which made the man angry, so he killed it. The elephant and its calf used the waterhole and made the water muddy. The cow couldn't drink. The Dorobo was angry, so he killed the elephant. But the calf escaped and found a Maasai man called Le-eyo. The elephant calf took Le-eyo back to the Dorobo's hut.

The god Naiteru-kop came down and told the Dorobo to get up early the next morning to make a compound and to find a calf and sacrifice it. Le-eyo overheard this, so he got up earlier and made a compound and a sacrifice. A leather cord came down from heaven, and a herd of cattle

---

[6] Another version of the story gives the snake a name: Tyanaba.)

started to come down the rope into the enclosure. The Dorobo cattle came out of their compound and mixed with the others. Since the Dorobo had no way of proving which were his, Le-eyo took them all. Since then, the Dorobo have been hunters, and the Maasai have herded cattle.

It is an interesting story since the rope from heaven resembles many African creation stories, but the "world on a rope" motif is also rather reminiscent of Jack and the Beanstalk.

In Rwanda, a similar tale is told about Gihanga, one of the early kings of Rwanda. He discovered that cows came out of a lake and set off with his men to capture them. However, having been warned by his diviners not to take his son, Gafomo, he sent his son off on an errand. Gafomo was suspicious and followed his father's expedition in secret. When they arrived at the lake, Gafomo hid in a tree.

Gihanga's men captured many of the cows that came up out of the lake. But when the bull came out, Gafomo was frightened and cried out. The bull turned back into the lake with the rest of the cows.

The San, however, have a different story to tell. In the old days, King Mamba, the snake, owned all the cattle. Heise was a friend of King Mamba's, but nothing he could do would get the king to give him even a single cow. So, Heise built a big fire and dared King Mamba to jump over it. To show him, Heise jumped first, easily clearing the fire and landing on the other side of it with a thump.

King Mamba was rather arrogant and thought he could do anything better than this puny human, so he gathered his coils together and leaped straight into the middle of the fire. Snakes are not good at jumping, after all. Once Heise saw the mamba completely burned to ashes, he grabbed the cows!

Animals are found in Egyptian mythology too. For instance, the great snake Apep inhabits the night world and tries to stop the sun god Ra from sailing his boat toward morning. Apep is a force of evil or disorder. However, the snake goddess Wadjet is the protector of Lower Egypt. She's often shown on the front of the pharaoh's crown to symbolize her protection of the land and its ruler.

The hippopotamus is also prevalent. Usually, the hippopotamus was seen as a dangerous creature belonging to the watery marshes, a symbol of disorder and destruction. The pharaoh was often shown harpooning a hippo, which was a sign of his mission to maintain order in the land. But the goddess Taweret shows the positive side of the hippopotamus: the mother's protectiveness.

There is a Nigerian tale that tells why the hippopotamus lives in the water. Once, the hippos lived on land like other animals. The Hippo King was second only to the Elephant King, and he had seven big, fat, wonderful wives. He was a generous host, always giving huge feasts.

At one of these feasts, the Hippo King stopped his guests from sitting down. "None of you even know my name," he said, "but you come and eat here nonetheless."

(This was true. Only his seven wives knew his name, and they weren't telling.)

So, the guests went away ashamed. All except Tortoise.

"If I find out your name, what will you do?" Tortoise asked the Hippo King.

"I'd be so ashamed if you did. I'd have to go and hide in the river!"

Now, Tortoise knew that the king and his wives all went down to the river in the morning to bathe. So, he dug a hole in the middle of the path they took and hid under the sand. Four of the wives passed by with the king, and Tortoise popped up right in front of the fifth wife, who stubbed her toe on his hard shell.

"Ow!" she howled. "Isantim, come and help me!"

The king came lumbering back to see what was the matter, but he didn't see Tortoise, who had dug back underneath the sand.

A month later, the Hippo King had another feast. He laid out excellent food and huge jars full of palm wine and invited everyone to partake freely.

But Tortoise shouted out, "I know your name, Isantim!"

And the hippopotamus had to go and live in the river, along with his seven cumbersome but lovely wives. They may come out of the river at night, but they're too ashamed to come out in the daytime!

Although real creatures like elands, snakes, elephants, and cows appear in African myths, Africa also has plenty of mythical creatures. Some are monsters (they'll get a chapter to themselves later), but some are benevolent, like Chipfalamfula, the "River-Shutter," a big fish who is said to have the ability to control a river's flow. He can cause floods, but he also saves drowning people. In one story from Mozambique, he saved a little girl by letting her climb down into his belly when she was nearly drowning in the water. Later, the same girl was pursued by ogres on land. Seeing this, Chipfalamfula sent a great wave to drown the ogres, and the girl got away.

Chapter 5: Trickster Tales

African trickster tales are very popular. Trickster tales are not purely African, of course; Native Americans tell tales about Coyote, Raven, and Nanabozho the Hare, and Japan has a trickster fox, Kitsune. The Vikings had the trickster god Loki, who tries to get Odin out of a fix by stealing the gold from the Rhine, and you may have read Br'er Rabbit tales when you were a child.

Why so many African trickster tales? Again, the answer is not necessarily that they make up an unusually high percentage of oral tradition (though it seems three out of every five Yoruba folk tales are trickster tales). Instead, it seems that they are highly appealing. Everyone likes a trickster tale, particularly when it tells of a tiny creature or a deprived individual getting ahead by using their wits and perhaps a little white lie or two. Sometimes, the tricksters are smart, small animals; sometimes, they're human. Tortoise, Hare, Jackal, Spider, and Gazelle are often trickster animals. Tricksters may be greedy, gluttonous, buffoonish, or even (like Legba) sexually insatiable.

In many Yoruba tales, Tortoise, Ijapa, is the trickster hero. He does some things that look pretty stupid. For instance, he once challenged the Hippopotamus to a game of tug of war. A tortoise is never going to win against such a huge animal! But, of course, Tortoise knew that. The fact is he had already got Elephant to agree to pull on the other end of the rope. Naturally, Tortoise won!

But Tortoise is greedy too. One tale tells how when his wife was trying to get pregnant, Tortoise visited an herbalist. The herbalist cooked up a fantastically tasty-smelling broth and put it in a calabash. "Give this to your wife," the herbalist said. "And don't be tempted to eat it yourself."

Tortoise started on his way with the calabash on his back, but that broth smelled so good. It was spicy, it was meaty, and he found he was going more and more slowly until, at long last, temptation got the better of him. Tortoise wolfed down the entire contents of the calabash without leaving any for his wife.

It tasted great. Of course, he had to tell a few little white lies to his wife, but Tortoise is a great liar, so that wasn't a problem.

Except that a few weeks later, he noticed his tummy was getting bigger and rounder day by day. You guessed it: Tortoise was pregnant. Even Tortoise would have difficulty explaining *that* to his wife.

Tortoise, like a lot of people who think they're smart, can also be really dumb at times. One day, he decided he wanted to collect all the knowledge in the world in a calabash and hang it up on a tree where no one else could get it. But he tied the calabash in front of him, and he couldn't manage to get up the tree.

Then, a little kid started laughing. "Just tie the calabash behind you, stupid!" he shouted. "Don't you know anything?"

Tortoise was so angry he threw the calabash down and smashed it. A good thing too; otherwise, none of us would know anything at all.

In a story from the Tsonga people, two tricksters go up against each other. Hare and Tortoise steal sweet potatoes from a farmer. They get a big pile of potatoes, but Hare starts to worry that the farmer will catch them.

"Why don't you go and check to make sure the farmer's not around?" he asks Tortoise.

Tortoise is immediately suspicious. Why does Hare want him out of the way? He thinks about it, and he tells Hare that there are two ways into the field. So, if he checks one, Hare needs to check the other, or else they could still get caught.

Hare thinks this is fine. He's faster than Tortoise, so he will be back to take all the potatoes for himself before Tortoise even reaches the gate. Off he goes, as fast as he can run.

Tortoise doesn't check the other gate. Tortoise climbs into Hare's bag and hides.

Hare checks the gate and comes back. Tortoise is nowhere to be seen. "Ha, ha! The potatoes are all mine!" he says. Hare starts chucking the potatoes into the bag. Then, he picks up the bag, and off he goes with all the potatoes. He won't have to share with Tortoise!

Meanwhile, Tortoise is inside the sack, methodically chomping his way through the tasty sweet potatoes. This story proves that the hare doesn't always beat the tortoise.

Perhaps the best-known African trickster is Anansi the spider from the Ashanti tradition. There's a lot of respect for *Kwaku Anansi*, Father Anansi, who is something of a cultural hero as well as a trickster. Sometimes, he works as a messenger for the supreme god Nyame, and he is also the creator of the sun, moon, stars, day, and night. Anansi brings rain and taught people how to sow grain. Although he can be too smart for his own good—like Tortoise, he tried to corral all the world's knowledge but couldn't climb up the tree—he's admired for his ingenuity and wisdom.

However, some Anansi tales are sheer slapstick. Once, he was hungry, but the farmer wouldn't give him any beans. He went to play with the farmer's children, but they wouldn't give him any beans either. So, he went away and covered himself in gum and then came back and rolled around on the ground with the children. He was soon covered in beans, which had stuck to the gum. Anansi went home to pick them off him and put them in a pot.

On another occasion, Anansi decided he wanted to own all the stories that have ever been told. Nyame owned the stories, but he was prepared to sell them to Anansi. The price was a high one: Anansi had to deliver Mmoboro (the hornets), Onini (the python), and Osebo (the leopard) to Nyame.

A spider against a swarm of hornets is not an even match. But Anansi was up for the challenge. He took a big gourd with a stopper. Then, he jumped in the water and got thoroughly wet. Next, he passed by the hornets' nest.

"What's up with you?" the hornets asked. "You're soaked!"

"A big storm's coming," Anansi answered. Then, he gave a start as if he'd just thought of something. "Hey, you should get in this gourd. It's much more waterproof than your nest."

Of course, once the hornets were in the gourd, he put the stopper in, and that was that.

Next was the python. Again, in a spider and python battle, the odds are that the spider will lose. But Anansi came equipped with a long bamboo stick. (What's this? Is he going to propose a pole-jump competition?)

Anansi stood there with the stick and looked at the snake. He looked back at the stick. Then, he told Onini, "My wife cut this stick, and she said, 'Hey, this pole is longer than the python!' And I think she's right!"

Onini was angry. The stick didn't look very long to him, and he told Anansi so. Anansi told him that no, he *still* thought the stick was longer. So, Onini stretched himself along the bamboo to show how long he was.

Anansi pointed out that snakes are wiggly, and bamboo grows straight, so he'd need to tie the python to the pole in a few places to make sure the measurement was right. Onini, suspecting nothing, said, "Okay, but make it quick."

So, that was that.

But a leopard? How could a spider manage to capture something like that?

Well, Anansi dug a pit and disguised it with branches. Then, it was just a matter of waiting for Osebo to fall in.

But how was Anansi going to get the leopard he'd trapped to Nyame? That was the deal, after all.

Anansi approached the edge of the pit and bent over. "Hello," he said in a friendly way. "What's all this? Has someone fallen in this hole?"

The leopard was furious, lashing his tail, but he calmed down when Anansi suggested a way to help him out. Anansi had a rope with him, and if Osebo could just tie the end to his tail, he could drag him out of the hole.

But Anansi had already tied the other end of the rope to a springy tree that he'd bent down. So, when the leopard got the rope around its tail, Anansi let go of the tree, and the leopard flew up into the air. He was trapped!

Even then, Nyame didn't want to give the tales away. Some people say he asked Anansi to catch a bush spirit. Anansi thought for a long time. It was impossible. Surely it was impossible? And then he had an idea.

Off Anansi went to the bush with a doll, a pot of sticky glue, and his breakfast. He found a tree where the bush spirits liked to hang out and set the doll under the tree. Anansi tipped the glue all over the doll, and then he put his breakfast in front of the doll and hid behind the tree. Soon enough, a bush spirit happened by.

"Hello," said Anansi from his hidey-hole. "Would you like some breakfast?"

"Thank you kindly," said the bush spirit, who sat down with the doll and began to eat. Soon, the bush spirit had finished its breakfast. Politely, it said, "Thank you." The doll said nothing.

"Good day to you," said the bush spirit. And still the doll said nothing.

"You might wish me a good day," grumbled the bush spirit. The doll still said nothing.

The bush spirit was getting pretty angry now. And the doll just kept looking at it with what was surely an insolent stare. So, the bush spirit slapped its face. Its hand stuck to the doll. It tried to pull away, but it couldn't, so it pushed the doll in the stomach with its foot—and its foot stuck to the doll too.

Once the bush spirit was tightly glued, Anansi took it back to Nyame. And so, all the stories ever told now belong to Anansi.

Once, there was a famine where Anansi lived. He could see an island offshore with a huge palm tree. But how could he reach it? His boat was broken and old. Still, Anansi decided to try. Six times the waves pushed him back to shore, but the seventh time, he made it through the breakers and got to the island, where he climbed up the tree and plucked the palm nuts.

Being lazy, he thought it would be easier to throw them down into the boat than carry all the nuts. However, every single nut fell in the water, not the boat! Anansi threw himself into the water in despair, but instead of sinking and drowning, he found himself in front of a house on the seabed. There, he met old man Thunder. After hearing Anansi's sad story, he gave him a pot.

"All you need to do," Thunder told Anansi, "is to tell the pot to do for you what it used to do for its master."

Anansi tried it out as soon as he got to shore. "Pot, pot," he said, "what you did for your master do for me." The pot instantly produced all kinds of good food and drink for him, and he ate it all up. And then Anansi thought of his hungry family. He could use the pot to feed them.

But there were a lot of them, and the magic might run out. If he kept the pot for himself, he could eat well every single day. So, he hid the pot and only used it when he was alone.

Unfortunately, the family noticed that Anansi was getting fatter while the rest of them were starving. His son Kweku Tsin decided to follow Anansi to find out why. Kweku Tsin had a superpower. He could turn himself into a fly, so he was easily able to follow his father without Anansi suspecting anything. He saw Anansi take the pot from its hiding place and make a pig of himself, eating everything it could produce. Then, he buzzed off to let the whole family in on the secret.

Once Anansi had gone off for the day, Kweku Tsin fetched the pot. "Pot, pot," he said, as he'd heard Anansi say. "What you did for your master do for me." And the pot gave the family as much food as it could. But it overheated because there were so many mouths to feed, and it stopped working. Kweku Tsin hid it again. The next time Anansi used the pot, it had no magic.

Anansi went to Thunder's house again. This time, it was much easier to get past the breakers. Thunder listened carefully to Anansi's story, which was a slightly edited one, and then gave Anansi a stick.

"It works just the same way as the pot," Thunder said. "Just tell it to do for you what it does for me."

But a pot is a pot, and a stick is a stick. When Anansi said, "Stick, stick, what you did for your master, do for me," the stick started beating him. It beat him black and blue before he finally managed to get hold of it and throw it back into the sea.

Kweku Tsin was actually smarter than his father Anansi. He discovered all the best hunting places, but he wouldn't tell his father where they were. Anansi tracked him by making a little hole in his hunting bag and putting ashes in it. The next time Kweku Tsin went hunting, Anansi just followed the trail of ash. Knowing all the best hunting spots, Anansi got there first the next day and warned Kweku Tsin off. "This is my hunting land now," Anansi said.

Kweku Tsin worked out how he had been tricked and decided to get some revenge. Knowing that Anansi would go to sell the meat and animal skins at the market, Kweku Tsin got to the main crossroads and set up a tiny image with bells around its neck high in a tree. He attached a long string to this image and then hid in the bush. When Anansi arrived, Kweku Tsin made the little image jump and dance by pulling on the string.

"The gods are angry," Anansi thought. "I had better give this god some meat."

But the god was not happy. Anansi gave it some more meat.

The god was still not happy. It wasn't happy until Anansi had given it all the meat and run away. Kweku Tsin took the meat to sell. He got rich, and eventually, he held a big feast. He told the story of his cunning and how he had beaten Anansi. Anansi was so ashamed that he promised to give up his cheating and tricks. (Naturally, that didn't last long, but that's another story!)

Sometimes, tricksters are associated with the work of creation. Remember that Anansi helped Nyame. Another spider, Ture, helped people acquire water and fire, according to the stories of the Zande people in central Africa.

An old woman grew yams and built a dam to corral all the water in the world. When people passed her hut, she would offer them yams but nothing to drink, so they would choke on the dry yams. When they choked, she would kill them.

Ture went to find the water behind the dam and filled up his gourd with as much water as he could. Then, he cut a hollow reed to use as a straw so he could suck the water out secretly. And then he went past the old woman's hut.

She offered him a yam. He ate it, and when she wasn't looking, he took a quick sip of water so he didn't choke. He had another yam. His secret water supply prevented him from choking. He had another yam. And another. He ate all the yams, and then he ran to the dam and broke it down, letting the water out so that it could run across the fields. This is why there is water in the world.

The blacksmith clan used to be the only people who had fire. They wouldn't let anyone else have it. Ture decided this was not right, so he went to the blacksmiths for a visit. Before he went, he dressed himself in old bark cloth, which was very fragile and very dry. When he sat by the blacksmiths' fire, the bark cloth caught fire, and he ran away, taking the secret of fire with him.

But Ture, like other tricksters, could be foolish. He was supposed to be hunting termites for food but seduced his mother-in-law while he was out in the bush instead. His wife was furious when he came home with no termites. That wasn't a problem for Ture; he told her a tall tale about how things had gone wrong.

Unfortunately, at this point, Ture's penis decided to speak up for itself. When it told the truth about what Ture had done, his wife was even more furious.

Another animal trickster is Agemo, a chameleon who carries messages for the Yoruba god Olorun. Once, the sea goddess Olokun boasted that she could weave better than Olorun. The god decided to send Agemo to check out that claim.

Every time Olokun brought out a cloth, Agemo walked on the cloth and managed to change his color to match it. She started trying more and more complex patterns and designs, but when he managed to repeat the pattern exactly on even her most complicated weave, she gave up.

"If I can't even beat the messenger," she lamented, "how can I ever beat his master?"

Malian hunters tell a tale about Sirankomi the great hunter. He never came back from the bush without a kill. The animals were worried he would kill them all, so they sent the buffalo disguised as a woman to learn his secrets.

Sirankomi fell for it. The buffalo-woman seduced him, and he took her to his hut, where she learned all his tricks. Sirankomi could transform himself into a termite mound, a stump, or a tuft of grass so the animals couldn't see him. But as they were talking, Sirankomi's mother passed the hut and warned the hunter not to give his secrets away to a one-night woman.

The next day, the buffalo-woman asked Sirankomi to accompany her to her own compound. She had told the other animals the secrets, so when Sirankomi became a termite mound, the warthogs dug it up with their tusks. When he became a tree stump, the elephants ripped it up. When he became a tuft of grass, all the grass-eating animals started munching away on him.

But because he had heard his mother's warning, Sirankomi had one trick left. He turned himself into a dust devil and whirled away home.

Another hunter-trickster is the Khoi-Khoi (Bushman) hero Heitsi-eibib, who was both a trickster and a shape-changer. He was born from a cow and grew into a mighty bull. He ran away when he saw the butcher coming to kill him and turned himself into a man. When the butcher arrived, he found Heitsi-eibib carving gourds.

"Have you seen a bull?"

"What bull?"

Having escaped the pot himself didn't make him a vegetarian. When he found that a village was going to slaughter a cow, he turned himself into a huge pot. They cooked the meat, but Heitsi-eibib drank up all the fat so that the meat left in the pot was dry and tasteless.

On his travels, he met ogres who killed all their visitors. The first, Gama-Gorib, challenged Heitsi-eibib to wrestle. Gama-Gorib knocked his opponent into a great pit, where he would perish. However, Heitsi-eibib told the hole to lift him up so that he could carry on fighting. Eventually, he knocked Gama-Gorib into the hole, and the ogre died. The next, Han-Gai-Gaib (also known as Ga-Gorib in some versions), used to challenge visitors to throw a stone at him. However, the stone was magic and would rebound and kill the person who threw it. So, Heitsi-eibib told Han-Gai-Gaib to close his eyes while he threw the stone. Instead of throwing the stone, he bashed Han-Gai-Gaib on the head and killed him.

Many tricksters are child prodigies. The Zulus tell the story of Uhlakanyana, who cut his own umbilical cord with his father's spearhead and announced his own arrival. Like many tricksters, Uhlakanyana was greedy, and he often got caught.

For instance, one time, an ogre caught him stealing the birds from his hunting nets. The ogre was getting ready to eat Uhlakanyana raw, but he persuaded the ogre he would taste better cooked. The ogre took him home and gave him to his mother to cook.

"You have to get the water just right," said Uhlakanyana. "I don't think it's hot enough."

"No?"

"Why don't you test it?"

The ogress stuck one finger in.

"That's not enough," Uhlakanyana said. "You have to get in the pot to see if it's hot enough."

Foolishly, the ogress got in the pot, and Uhlakanyana slammed the lid down and ran away.

Another story shows how Uhlakanyana "traded up." Uhlakanyana found a tasty root and took it home to his mother to cook while he went to a wedding. However, she tasted it and liked it and then tasted it again until she ate it all.

Uhlakanyana complained, so she gave him a gourd.

He walked past some boys who were milking their cow, but they didn't have a pot. So, he lent them the gourd. But they broke it, and he complained. So, they gave him a little hunting spear. He went on his way.

Next, he walked past some boys who were trying to cut meat, but they didn't have a knife. So, he lent them the spear, but one of them broke it. He complained, so they gave him an ax, and off he went.

As he walked, he met some women collecting firewood, but they didn't have an ax. So, he lent them his, but one of the women broke the handle. He complained. They had a blanket, so they gave him that.

Later on, he met two hunters sleeping naked on the ground and offered to lend them the blanket. But they slept badly and, having nightmares, managed to tear the blanket. Uhlakanyana complained, and they gave him a big shield, and he walked on.

A little later, he saw some hunters who had cornered a leopard. But it was hissing and striking out with its claw, and they couldn't get close enough to kill it. So, he lent them the shield. They killed the leopard but broke the handle on the shield.

Now Uhlakanyana was really cross.

"You broke the handle of the shield that was given to me by the hunters who tore my blanket, which the women gave me when they broke my ax, which the boys gave me who broke my spear, which the boys gave me who broke my gourd, which my mother gave me after she ate my dinner while I was away at a wedding."

This story must have impressed the hunters because they gave him a huge war spear, and he took it home.

Not all trickster stories are fun. The Bakongo story of Moni Mambu is tough and unpalatable. First, he found two brothers who never quarreled; one was a fisherman, and the other tapped palm trees to make wine. Moni Mambu put the fish traps on the palm trees and the calabashes in the water, and the two brothers came to blows. Moni Mambu laughed to see them fighting.

Then, he visited a village and asked for hospitality. A woman said to him, "You can eat peanut stew with my children for lunch." He took her words literally; he roasted the children and ate the peanut stew with the meat.

Moni Mambu went hunting with the chief. The chief said, "Shoot everything that moves. I don't want anything left but the slugs and snails." So, Moni Mambu shot the lizards, birds, snakes, antelopes, hunting dogs, children, and the chief's favorite wife.

The chief condemned Moni Mambu to death, but he said he could only be killed one way: by drowning. The people carried him to the river with a big fish trap to drown him in, but on the way, Moni Mambu managed to convince a stranger that he was a ritual priest and that he was waiting with the fish trap to anoint a king. The stranger, who thought being king would be great, got in the fish trap. Moni Mambu slammed the lid on him and escaped. The stranger was drowned instead.

Moni Mambu eventually came to a bad end. He found a talking skull, and he was so excited he told the elders of the village. They went to see the skull, but it wouldn't talk to the elders, so they accused Moni Mambu of lying to them and killed him.

Next, let's take a look at Eshu, a Yoruba god who is a bit more than a trickster but is definitely tricky. (Many of the tales told of Eshu are also told of his counterpart Legba.) For a start, Eshu is the god of chance, luck, accidents, and the unpredictability of life. He is also Olorun's messenger on earth, and he is the god of the crossroads and divination.

Once upon a time, there were two men who were the very best of friends. They were so happy that they said their friendship would last forever. But Eshu overheard them.

The next day, the two friends saw a man pass them as they worked on their farms. Later, when they were sitting under a tree and chatting, one of them mentioned the friendly greeting the man in the red hat gave them.

"Red?" the other man said. "It was black!"

"I'm not blind! It was red!"

They got more and more heated, and in the end, they came to blows over the issue.

Eshu actually had passed between the two of them while wearing a hat that was black on one side and red on the other. He tricked them into having that argument. Why? Because their idea of a forever friendship was boastful and proud, and he wanted to show them that life is all about change and chance.

A less well-known trickster comes from the Arabic stories of *One Thousand and One Nights* via Zanzibar, a trading post where Arabs not only traded but also settled and intermarried with the Swahili-speaking locals. Abu Nuwas got himself thoroughly naturalized as a trickster living in an urban environment and living by his wits.

For instance, when Abunuwasi (as he's known in Zanzibar) borrows a big saucepan from his neighbor, he returns it along with a much smaller pan.

"What's this?" his neighbor asks. "I only lent you one saucepan."

"Oh," says Abunuwasi. "I think the big saucepan must have been pregnant when you lent it to me. This is its baby."

Now, the neighbor thinks Abunuwasi is not the brightest cookie, but he's quite happy to have an extra saucepan. However, Abunuwasi isn't as dumb as he looks.

Next time he needs to borrow the big saucepan, he keeps it. After a few months, the neighbor is worried about where the saucepan is.

"Remember that big saucepan?" he asks Abunuwasi.

Abunuwasi bursts out crying. He sobs and sobs. He cries real tears.

"The saucepan died," he wails.

"Saucepans don't die," says the neighbor angrily. "Don't be so stupid."

Abunuwasi looks at his neighbor. "You believed me when I told you the saucepan had a baby, didn't you? And if they are born, they can die."

Abunuwasi even outsmarted the sultan. The sultan had given Abunuwasi a beautiful young wife along with a present of a thousand gold pieces. Abunuwasi and his wife were blissfully happy for a little while, but then the money ran out. It's difficult to be happy when you are hungry.

So Abunuwasi thought of a plan. He went to the sultan, weeping, and said his wife had died. What was worse, he had no money for the funeral. The sultan gave him his sympathy and, more to the point, twenty gold pieces.

At the same time, Abunuwasi's wife went to the sultan's wife and said that Abunuwasi had died and that he had been such a bad husband that there was no money left to bury him with. The sultana gave the girl her commiserations and twenty gold pieces.

When the sultan had dinner with his wife, he mentioned how Abunuwasi's wife had died and what a pity it was that Abunuwasi couldn't find any happiness in life.

"You've got it wrong," his wife said. "It's Abunuwasi who died. I saw his wife this morning."

So, they decided they had better find out who was right. They sent a servant to Abunuwasi's house. Abunuwasi made his wife hide under a sheet. "Don't breathe," he warned her. Then, he showed the servant his "dead" wife.

The sultana wasn't happy. She sent her own messenger to the house. Abunuwasi's wife recognized the girl who had been sent, so she got Abunuwasi to lie under the sheet. It was his turn to play dead.

The sultan and his wife were now thoroughly confused. They couldn't trust their own servants to tell them the truth, so they decided to set out to Abunuwasi's house together. Of course, the sultan was always preceded by his drummers and horsemen, so Abunuwasi had plenty of notice. Both Abunuwasi and his wife got under the sheet this time. When the sultan and his wife came into the house, they immediately saw the two "dead" bodies.

"This is a mystery," said the sultan. "It needs clearing up. I'll give a thousand gold pieces to anyone who can tell me what's going on."

The "dead" Abunuwasi sat up and shouted, "You're on! Give me the gold, and I'll explain!"

Chapter 6: Monsters and Mythical Beasts

If you look at a medieval map, you'll see Africa is full of monsters: unicorns, griffins, basilisks, and manticores, as well as elephants, crocodiles, and lions. There were men who had no heads and men with only one huge foot, which they used as an umbrella (though they were found in India too, according to the texts). For medieval Europeans, Africa was a fascinating but dangerous place. They knew about it mainly from texts written by the Greeks and Romans since very few Westerners had actually been there. Europeans let their imaginations run riot. However, as we know today, Africa is not like that.

Still, Africa has its own monsters, although they are very different from the ones that medieval monks drew so carefully. In fact, the monks were completely wrong about one thing: they missed the legendary vampires. And there are a *lot* of vampires in Africa.

For instance, there's the adze, which lives in Togo and Ghana. It looks like an innocent firefly, but it can transform into human shape. It can also possess people, making them into witches (*abasom*). The adze sucks blood from people as they sleep, and it's particularly dangerous since, in its firefly form, it can creep through cracks in walls or under doors. Its favorite victims are children with their sweet young blood.

If that makes you think of mosquitoes, you may be right; some scholars speculate that the adze might have been created as a metaphor for malaria. Make sure you sleep indoors in a well-protected place, and you'll be safe from both the adze and the bugs.

The Asanbosam, or Sasabonsam, is another vampire, which terrifies the Akan people of Ghana. It lives in trees and attacks from above. It has iron teeth, iron hooks instead of feet and hands, and bat wings, just like Count Dracula. The Asanbosam are spirits of the forest who defend the woods against humans. One should not go into the wild forest on Thursday, which is a day set aside for the forest to renew itself, or they will hunt you down. Basically, the Asanbosam is a moral guardian, ensuring that people keep the rules that allow the ecosystem to function properly. Nineteenth-century missionaries, of course, missed that point and instead interpreted the Asanbosam to be the Christian Devil.

The Ramanga of Madagascar blends a rather nasty reality with a scary myth. The myth says that the Ramanga is a vampire that eats nail clippings and drinks blood. However, the reality is that there was a class of ritual practitioners whose job was to ensure that witches could not get hold of the blood, nail clippings, or saliva of their chieftains to work evil magic on. There was only one way to do this, and that was to eat the nail clippings and suck up any blood that was spilled (for instance, in a hunting accident).

It's interesting how, now that most of the Betsileo tribe are Christian and no longer believe in such witchcraft, a monster more akin to the Western idea of a vampire has emerged.

In Ashanti folklore, the obayifo is both a vampire and a witch, which is quite a common pairing in African myth. It can inhabit any human body and is obsessed with food. You can recognize an obayifo by the light that shines from their armpits and anus. Obayifo can shapeshift and fly, and it can also possess animals; for instance, one could possess a bull and make it kill people in a blind rage.

Women who practice witchcraft often turn into obayifo. They like to suck children's blood and can travel great distances by night. But the obayifo can be deterred by putting a plate of raw meat at the entrance to the village; they will eat that and come no farther into the settlement. Ashanti people will also share a little food with others in case the person asking for food is an obayifo. If you give food to an obayifo, it will keep its teeth out of you.

There are also a number of cannibal stories. The Fulani tell how Debbo Engal had ten daughters and how each daughter took a lover so she could suck his blood. Bantus terrify their children with the story of

Tshikashi Tshikulu, the old woman of the forest who stalks women and children to eat them.

Apart from man-eaters and blood drinkers, Africa has various kinds of aquatic monsters. The Gbahali, for instance, is Liberia's version of Scotland's Loch Ness Monster; it's a huge crocodile-like creature that is said to live in rainforest rivers and ambush its prey. It can grow up to thirty feet long. Some people have suggested it bears a resemblance to the dinosaur *Postosuchus*, which died out two hundred million years ago. But no one appears to have seen one for a while; maybe it was just a big crocodile, after all.

Ninki Nanka is another legendary reptile that lives in the West African swamps. It comes out at night to hunt down and devour whatever it can find. Accounts of it vary; it is a dragon, it has a horse's head, it is thirty feet long, or it is as long as a palm tree is tall. It is unimaginably huge, or it looks like a python with a feathery crest and mirror-like scales. Maybe it was originally a pre-Islamic snake god, but nowadays, it's more often used as a bogeyman to scare children and keep them from wandering outside the village. Some Gambians, particularly in the towns, think it is a myth or has become extinct, while others are not so sure. At least one national park ranger claims to have seen it. The big problem in finding evidence is that when people see the Ninki Nanka, they usually die shortly afterward, so there are few living witnesses.

Another "Loch Ness Monster" is the Inkanyamba, a legendary snake, eel, or water monster said to live, among other places, at Howick Falls in KwaZulu-Natal Province, South Africa. According to the Xhosa, only sangomas (traditional healers) are able to approach the falls safely. The Inkanyamba is associated with rain and is said to be able to leave the water in the shape of a tornado or waterspout. The Inkanyamba is actually more of a god than a monster; remember, many other gods are associated with serpents (such as Lebe or Ala with her royal python).

The forests of central Africa are defended by the Biloko (plural; one of them is called an Eloko). These dwarf-like forest-dwellers are ancestor spirits that defend their hunting grounds ferociously. They live in hollow trees, dress in leaves, and ring little bells that cast a spell on anyone who hears them. (Fortunately, a talisman or fetish can be effective against this magic.) If this doesn't make them sound particularly vicious, you should know they will eat people if they can.

There is a tale about a woman who made her husband take her hunting. He had a hut in the forest that he used on his expeditions, and he left her there while he went to check his snares. He warned her about the Biloko and their little bells and told her to keep the door tightly shut and open to nobody but him.

However, when the woman heard the bells ringing, she forgot all about his warning and let an Eloko into the hut. When the hunter came back, he found only her bones.

Another animal of the Congo is something of a mystery. The Abada is similar to the West's unicorn since its horns are an antidote against poison and have other healing powers. The only difference is that, unlike the unicorn, the Abada has two horns and apparently is more the size of a donkey than a horse.

It is also known as the Nillekma, under which name it was noted in the Zoological Journal of 1829. However, there is not much information on the creature available, and it is possible that the Abada is not a monster at all and just an ordinary antelope. It is, according to one account, very tasty to eat.

Go to Ethiopia today, and you'll be lucky to find anyone who knows about the Ethiopian Pegasus. However, the Roman naturalist Pliny the Elder (who, incidentally, was a martyr to science, having decided to stay in Pompeii to observe the eruption of Mount Vesuvius up close) tells us all about this creature. According to him, they were winged horses with two horns, and they didn't actually come from Ethiopia; they bred on an island off the shore of Eritrea.

Although Pliny was, in some regards, a good scientist, he was too willing to believe travelers' tales and urban myths. This was exacerbated when medieval monks got hold of his works and used them as the basis for bestiaries, collections of what was known about the animal world. If you're looking for an Ethiopian Pegasus, your best bet is to find a library with a good collection of medieval illuminated manuscripts.

Another Congo inhabitant is perhaps more celebrated outside Africa. Kongamato, "breaker of boats," appears in the video game *Final Fantasy XIV*. The Kaonde people described this monster as a kind of pterosaur—a huge red-winged lizard—that enjoyed capsizing canoes and could cause a person to die by just looking at them. In the game, though, the Kongamato turns out to be a useful mount and can be summoned by using a special Kongamato whistle.

South Africa has two particularly interesting mythical animals. First is the impundulu, the lightning bird of the Zulu, which is often identified with the strange-looking hamerkop ("hammerhead"). It is a huge black and white bird that summons thunder and lightning.

While the impundulu is a natural phenomenon, its association with witches, who may pass the control of the bird down in their family, has helped to make it a bird of evil omen. It can be forced to become the servant of a witch, who can use it to attack her enemies, and it can also become a vampire that drinks human blood. It cannot be killed by any means except, oddly enough for a lightning bird, by fire.

Less noxious but still very annoying is the tikoloshe or tokoloshe, a mischievous spirit that has the power of invisibility. It's a common bogeyman that can be called on to scare children (he will bite off your toes when you're asleep, or so it is said). It can also cause severe illness or even the death of enemies. Unlike the impundulu, tokoloshe are easy to get rid of since any Christian pastor can banish them. They are also tiny little dwarves, so if you put your bed legs up on bricks, they can't do anything to you.

In urban South African culture, the tokoloshe has become a figure of fun like a gremlin or the Grinch; it appears in comic strips and is blamed for all kinds of common mishaps.

Let's finish this chapter with a story from the San people and their cultural hero Khaggen, "Mantis," who created the earth, the sky, and the animals. It shows how there is no distinction between the animal and human worlds to some African peoples, at least in myth.

Khaggen's daughter ran away to live with the snakes. His son, Cogaz, went to fetch her back, and she was willing to come but warned him that the snakes would try to bite them. So, they tied grass stalks around their legs to protect them, and that's how they got away from the snakes.

Khaggen was annoyed that the snakes had tried to bite his children, so he sent a flood to drown them. However, the chief of the snakes and his followers survived. Khaggen then struck them with his stick, and they became men.

Later, Khaggen heard about a group of giants that drank women's blood. He decided to send Cogaz to kill the giants, giving him one of his teeth to take with him. Cogaz found a woman being held prisoner by the giants and freed her, but the giants gave chase. To escape, Cogaz threw Khaggen's tooth on the ground, and it grew into a mountain. From the top of the mountain, Cogaz could shoot poisoned arrows. Realizing that Cogaz was in trouble, Khaggen decided to help. He cut his leather hunting bag into strips, which turned into dogs and chased away the giants.

When the baboons saw Cogaz collecting wood to make bows, they decided to kill him before he was able to use the bows. They hung his body up in a tree. Then, they sang songs that degraded Khaggen. However, when Khaggen arrived, they changed the words, hoping he hadn't heard what they had been singing. However, a baby baboon, which didn't know any better, carried on singing the old words. Khaggen was angry. He plugged up each baboon's backside with a wooden peg and banished them to the mountains, and that is why baboons have red backsides and live in the wilderness.

Khaggen secretly created an eland out of his son-in-law's discarded sandal by rubbing it with honey to make it grow. His son-in-law found out about it, and since the sandal was his, he reckoned the eland should be his too. So, he killed the eland for meat. Khaggen found the eland's gall, but it burst and covered him with foul-smelling mucus. Khaggen took an ostrich feather to clean himself, and when he had gotten rid of the gunk, he threw the feather up into the sky, where it became the moon.

Chapter 7: Heroes in African Myth

As well as gods and ancestors, Africa has an abundance of heroes. They quite often overlap with the other realms of myth, as well as with actual history. Some heroes have elements in their stories that are highly reminiscent of trickster stories, while Sunjata Keita is the archetypal hero of Mali but was also an actual historical figure.

The Kingdom of Luba in the southern Democratic Republic of Congo was founded in the 16th century and traces its origins back to Prince Kalala Ilunga.

The despot Nkongolo ruled in the Congo. He married his two daughters to a hunter from the east, Ilunga Mbidi Kiluwe, but after feeling threatened by the younger man, he chased Ilunga into exile. Ilunga's son, Kalala Ilunga, grew up in exile along with Mijubu wa Kalenga, the first diviner. Eventually, the young prince decided to go to take his place at his grandfather's court.

Nkongolo invited Kalala Ilunga to dance for him. However, Mijubu warned the boy that Nkongolo had dug a concealed pit and filled it with spears where Kalala Ilunga was supposed to dance. So, when Kalala Ilunga was called on, he uncovered the hidden pit with his own spear and then overthrew the tyrant Nkongolo.

Ever since then, the spear dance (*kutomboka*) has been performed at the end of every investiture of a new chief to commemorate the event.

Who is the hero of this story? Apparently, it depends on who is telling it; for some people, it's the young prince, but for others, it's the diviner, Mijubu wa Kalenga.

(By the way, Kalala Ilunga is said to have introduced advanced ironworking to the Luba. Finely made axes became symbols of power and prestige, though they are sometimes so ornate they might not have been usable as axes.)

In the bend of the Congo River, the Mongo have a hero who, like Kalala Ilunga, was on a mission for justice. Lianja's mother became pregnant and could not give birth for a long time. When she finally did, she bore a number of children, ants, birds, and whole tribes of men. Lianja refused to be born the normal way, saying that his mother's birth passage had already been used by too many people. Instead, he and his sister Nsongo were born from a wound made in their mother's thigh.

The wicked Sausau had killed Lianja's father, and even before Lianja's umbilical cord had been cut, Lianja started to make war on Sausau. First, he sent a swarm of flies and wasps, but Sausau protected himself with clouds of smoke. Then, he sent various clans of men, but Sausau killed their leaders, including Lianja's brother.

Finally, Lianja entered into single combat against Sausau. Sausau threw spears at Lianja. They went right through him but then flew back through the air toward Sausau. Lianja's wounds healed instantly, so Sausau hurled spear after spear without effect.

Eventually, Lianja grappled Sausau to the ground, asked Nsongo to give him his knife, and sawed Sausau's head off.

So far, this is a typical hero story, but now it takes an odd turn. Nsongo had fallen in love with Sausau. After being offered a reward by her brother for her part in the war, she asked him to bring Sausau back to life. So, Lianja did this and gave Sausau to his sister as a slave.

Lianja then brought all the dead soldiers on both sides back to life and, together with Nsongo, led them through the forest to the land that he had been promised.

Another tale tells how Lianja and Nsongo had to take refuge from an ogre in a baobab tree. The tree protected them, but the ogre called its friends to help. The ogres tore the tree's bark and branches before eventually giving up and going away. Before setting off again, Lianja healed the baobab tree. He is a hero who has both warlike and peaceful tendencies; in other words, he is a healer and a warrior.

Jeki la Njambe of the Duala in coastal Cameroon was a despised younger half-brother to eight other sons of his father, Njambe. His mother's only daughter had been stolen by a chimpanzee, and although she was heavily pregnant, she could not give birth. On one occasion, when she was made to stack firewood, Jeki jumped out of her womb to help her and then jumped back in again. Another time, all nine wives had been looking for shrimp in the coastal shallows, but the tide started coming in. Again, he jumped out of his mother's womb and rescued them all before jumping back inside.

Eventually, Jeki thought it was time to be born. Before he came out, his mother gave birth to woven cloths, metal ingots, musical instruments, amulets, a canoe, and finally Jeki himself, along with his own special amulet, Ngalo.

Jeki was hated by his father and brothers. His father tested him, showing him a big wooden chest and asking what was in it. Jeki would get a beating for each wrong answer. "Cloth," he said. No, it wasn't cloth, and all his half-brothers beat him. "Gold," he said next, but that was wrong too, so he was beaten again.

Finally, he gave the right answer, which he'd known all along: "A single louse from your head, father. Oh, and it's female." But now he knew just how much his brothers hated him.

A little later, Jeki was summoned by his father and told to wash a big wooden chest. When his father had come to power, he had summoned various magical animals and imprisoned them, and this became the secret of his power. In this chest was a ferocious leopard that he had imprisoned magically.

Jeki was about to open the chest, but his amulet Ngalo warned him not to, instead telling him to take the chest down to the river and wash the outside first. Jeki took the chest into the deep water and washed all around the outside. By the time he was ready to take it out of the river and clean the inside, the leopard had drowned.

Another of Njambe's magical defenses was a giant crocodile. He proposed a third test for Jeki. Jeki must bring the crocodile to him. Jeki took his canoe, which had been born just before he appeared from his mother's womb, and invited the crocodile politely to a council in the village. Then, he summoned up a great wave to wash the crocodile into the village, where it snapped up a few cows for breakfast before Njambe could get rid of it.

Finally, Njambe asked Jeki to climb the huge palm tree for nuts. Yet another magical creature, the vicious kambo bird, lived at the top of the palm tree. So, Jeki asked his half-brothers to climb the tree first, and they did. One after another was killed by the kambo bird. When they had all been killed, Jeki climbed the tree, protected by his amulet Ngalo, and collected the nuts. He caught the kambo bird and burned it to death.

Then, he found medicine and brought his brothers back to life.

Later, he went to the chimpanzee land to find his sister. The chimpanzees showed him dozens of lovely women, who all looked exactly the same, and told him to choose. Luckily, Ngalo had given Jeki good advice again. Jeki sent out a little bee, which was easily able to distinguish the real sister from the fakes.

Tragic heroes exist too. The story of Aruan is told in Benin. Aruan was one of two sons who were born to King Ozolua of the Kyama people on the same day. But Aruan did not cry out, whereas his half-brother Esigie did. Because of this, everyone thought Esigie had been born first, and he became the heir. Ozolua favored Aruan, though, and gave him a magical sword. Aruan was told to plant it in the ground where his capital would be. Ozolua wanted to be buried there when he died.

But Esigie tricked Aruan into planting the sword in a bad place. One of Aruan's servants dug a pit and filled it with his tears to create a huge lake. When Ozolua died, Esigie stole the body and buried it in Benin. Aruan went to war, wearing a bell on his breastplate. He told his servants that if they heard the bell, it meant he had lost, and they were to throw his entire household and all of his possessions into the lake.

Aruan won the war, but while he was celebrating his victory, the bell fell onto the ground and rang out. When he returned, he found his home devastated. Grieving, he threw himself into the lake and drowned.

The Fulani have a tale of another despised prince, Goroba-Dike, who was a younger son. He had no inheritance, so he disguised himself as a peasant and got a job working for a blacksmith.

Princess Kode Ardo declared she would only marry a man whose fingers were small enough for him to wear a tiny ring she had on her little finger. Many tried, but only Goroba-Dike could wear it. So, the princess had to marry the blacksmith's boy.

The king and all his warriors set off to make war with the Tuaregs, who had raided their cattle. Goroba-Dike went with them, riding on a donkey. However, when they left the city, he rode off in the wrong direction. Everyone laughed at him, particularly the king's other sons-in-law.

Secretly, Goroba-Dike transformed himself into a splendid horseman and rejoined the army. He told the king's sons-in-law that he would fight for them if they each gave him one of their ears, and they did so.

Goroba-Dike's wife, Kode Ardo, was kidnapped by the Tuaregs, and he rescued her, still wearing his splendid appearance. He had been wounded on the arm, and she used a piece of her dress to bandage the wound.

That night, he appeared back at court as a blacksmith's boy. Kode Ardo suddenly saw that her "peasant" husband had been wounded in exactly the same place as the splendid warrior and that his wound was tied up with the cloth she had given him. He told his story, but the sons-in-law were dismissive; they said he had invented it all.

So, he told the story of how the sons-in-law had each given him an ear. He showed the necklace of ears, and when the king looked at his sons-in-law, he saw that all of them except Goroba-Dike were missing one ear.

Kobe Ardo now knew she had a royal husband, and the king was so impressed that he handed over his entire kingdom to Goroba-Dike in gratitude.

Many of these heroes have an atypical birth and childhood. Aiwel Longar of the Dinka/Bor in Sudan is another enfant terrible. He was born when a river god heard an elderly widow weeping because she had no son. The god took pity on her and gave her a son. Aiwel Longar was born with a full set of teeth, which showed he would have great spiritual power. He was also already able to walk and talk. He instructed his mother to tell no one about his birth, or she would die, but she ignored his instruction. She died, so Aiwel went to live with his father, the river god, until he was grown.

When Aiwel returned to the village, he had an ox of every color and took over the cattle of his mother's dead husband. A drought came to the country, and while everyone else's cattle grew thin, Aiwel's cattle remained fat. When he touched the ground, water sprang up, and grass grew. Eventually, thanks to these gifts, he became the village headman. His spear was the sign of his divinity, and spearmaster priests still trace their origins from him and sacrifice oxen in his honor.

Unmarried women are often trouble in African stories. In many of these tales, women do not want to be single, and it's accepted that women are sexual creatures. But sometimes, they become heroes. Yennenga, the daughter of a king, was old enough to be married, but her father would not find her a husband. So, she found a partner for herself. However, the king was not pleased when she became pregnant, and he ordered her death. Her friends found out about his order and gave her a warning. Together, they stole horses from the royal stables and escaped. But Yennenga rode so hard that she had a miscarriage.

After many adventures and much riding, she came to the land of Rialle the elephant hunter. At first, Rialle believed Yennenga was a young man, as she was riding in men's clothes and her friends deferred to her as if she were a chieftain. But later, she told him the truth, and they were married. She called her son Stallion in memory of the horse whose speed saved her life. The royal house of the Mossi in Burkina Faso is thought to be descended from her.

A similar story is told by the Sereer people of Senegal about their aristocratic house of Guelowar. The Guelowar are matrilineal, with inheritance passing down the female line. How did that come about?

It happened when a Mande princess fell in love with a griot musician. Princesses and griots don't mix; they come from different classes. She knew her father would never let her marry the griot. But she was head over heels in love. When she became pregnant, she had to flee, and she ended up living in a cave by the edge of the ocean.

The king of that land heard of the beautiful woman in the cave and went to see for himself whether she was as beautiful as he'd heard. He fell in love immediately and asked her to marry him. She was pregnant and thought of her unborn child. She agreed to marry him if he made her child his heir. He agreed, and so she went with him.

When her child was born, it was a girl. The king immediately had it proclaimed that the infant's sons would rule the land after him, which is why the Guelowar still pass inheritance through the mother, not the father.

Finally, a different kind of hero is found in a delightful Shona story: a musician, one who played the mbira, or thumb piano as some people call it. He was the elder son of a poor father, and they had only saved enough for one son to marry. The younger son found himself a wife, so the elder son had to set off to find his fortune. He took his mbira with him to pass the time on his journey.

First, he came to the country of the hares, but they boxed his ears and would not let him pass. He couldn't go any farther, so he sat down and played his mbira. To his surprise, the hares started dancing to the music, and he was able to pass their country and go on his way.

Then, he had to pass through antelope country, but the antelopes threatened him with their twisty horns. Again, he sat down and played his mbira, and the antelopes began to dance. He moved on.

Then, he came upon a pride of lions, and they roared at him and showed their huge teeth. But now he had faith that his mbira would weave its magic, and so it did. The lions rolled about with their legs in the air and eventually went to sleep.

At last, the musician came to a lake, sat down to rest, and started playing just for his own pleasure.

But the water spirits that lived in the lake gathered around to listen and decided that the mbira player should play for their king. They took him down under the water to the king's palace, and he played in front of the royal court. The king loved the music and gave the young man a wife and a village in the underwater land.

The elder brother, still full of love for his family, went to tell them of the good fortune he had found, but his younger brother would not come. So, the mbira player went back under the lake, and no one has seen him since.

Chapter 8: Mythical and Legendary Kings and Queens

As the last chapter showed, there are varying degrees of "mythical," from outright invention to orally remembered history. Historians don't always agree on just how mythical these figures are. For instance, the Queen of Sheba might have been the queen of Yemen, which shared much of its culture with the Horn of Africa in early times and is not even in Africa. On the other hand, Akhenaten is definitely known from his own monuments, and you can see Ras Tafari's coronation on a newsreel from 1930.

Akhenaten was the tenth ruler of the Eighteenth Dynasty of Egypt. He came to the throne in 1353 BCE as Amenhotep IV but soon changed his name to Akhenaten, incorporating the name of the sun disk Aten. Aten became the patron god of his royal house, replacing Amun-Ra and all the other gods.

Akhenaten moved his capital to Amarna, where he patronized a new style of Egyptian art, which was more elongated and more realistic than the preceding styles. He made the royal family the unique link between Aten and the people, and reliefs show him, Nefertiti, and their daughters in intimate scenes of family life, not the hierarchical processions of earlier art.[7]

---

[7] Egyptian art rarely shows the male children of the king unless they have been given high office.

Akhenaten's reforms might have been intended to demonstrate the primacy of his particular god, weakening other priesthoods that were rival power sources to the pharaoh; however, many scholars believe his views came closer to monotheism.

His wife, **Nefertiti**, or Neferneferuaten Nefertiti in full, is well known for her majestic beauty. The bust of Nefertiti in the Berlin Museum is celebrated as one of the masterworks of Egyptian art, and her beauty contrasts strangely with the almost deformed depictions of her husband.

Nefertiti might not have been just a beautiful face. It's quite possible that she ruled in her own right. According to one interpretation of the evidence, five years before Akhenaten died, he made Nefertiti co-ruler of Egypt and renamed her Ankhkheperure Neferneferuaten. Upon his death, she took a new regnal name, reigning as Ankhkheperure Smenkhkare and acting as regent for her stepson, Tutankhamun.

Nefertiti must have been trying to keep her husband's dreams alive, but things began to fall apart. No one knows quite how, but the boy king Tutankhamun reintroduced the old gods, and when he died, Nefertiti's father Ay and then the general Horemheb ruled Egypt. Akhenaten's capital was lost under the sands, and his monuments were defaced. His name was erased from inscriptions, and king lists of later pharaohs make no mention of him.

Hatshepsut was another female pharaoh. She was the fifth pharaoh of the Eighteenth Dynasty. Egypt was then at the peak of its power, and Hatshepsut was at the top of the tree. She was the daughter of Thutmose I and the Great Royal Wife to her half-brother Thutmose II. Thutmose II died young in around 1479 BCE. On his death, her stepson became pharaoh as Thutmose III, and she took power first as regent (since he was only a child) and later as co-ruler. After Hatshepsut took power, she was depicted as a male pharaoh with a khat head cloth and a false beard.

Hatshepsut became a massive patron of building works in Thebes (Luxor) and elsewhere, particularly at Karnak and at Deir el-Bahari, where she built her own mortuary temple. She also funded a mission to the Land of Punt in the Horn of Africa; details of the expedition are shown in reliefs at Deir el-Bahari and show how the temple's forecourts were planted with rare frankincense trees from Punt.

Like Akhenaten, Hatshepsut suffered a campaign dedicated to wiping out her memory after her death. This might have been done by her stepgrandson Amenhotep II, whose claim to the throne was not particularly secure. It also might have been motivated by the desire to wipe out the memory of female rulers (and worse, from the patriarchal point of view, a successful female ruler).

Queen Amina was a Hausa queen of Zazzau, with its capital in the city of Zaria in Nigeria. She is a controversial figure. Some historians believe she is only a mythical figure, and folk legends of her rule may not reflect reality. She was born in the mid-16th century and was the daughter of the king of Zazzau. When her brother became king, she led his cavalry. (Women warriors are well evidenced in historical times, as you will see later in this chapter.)

When the king died, Amina took the throne herself. She refused to marry and set Zazzau on an expansionist program. At the time, there were seven different Hausa states; she moved against the other six and created a larger empire. There are stories of her taking a new lover in every city she conquered but having him executed the morning after so that he couldn't challenge her rule. That's *probably* not true.

Whatever the truth of her history, Amina has provided powerful inspiration for Black culture in the 21st century. She appears in the video game *Age of Empires III*, and her story is read by the newly literate Kingsley Smith to his family in Steve McQueen's film *Education*.

Kandake or Candace was not a name but the title given to queens (or rather queen mothers) of Kush. The Kushite Empire was based in the city of Meroe in Sudan, which was a wealthy trading center on the Nile. Succession was matrilineal; the king's sister became Kandake, and her son became the next ruler. The first Kandake to rule in her own right appears to have been Narhiqo, ruling around 170 BCE, and at least seven ruling Kandakes followed her over the years.

Kandake Amanirenas was one of the most famous. Born around 40 BCE, she led Kushite armies against the invading Romans and is mentioned by the Greek geographer Strabo, a contemporary. She was apparently blind in one eye, but this didn't stop her from being a formidable warrior and negotiating an advantageous peace with Rome. It wasn't until the later emergence of Aksum that the Kushite Empire disintegrated.

In the medieval Alexander romances, which often have remarkably little to do with the historical facts of Alexander the Great's campaigns, Candace is shown as the queen of Ethiopia and even marries Alexander. This follows the mention in the Bible of "Candace, queen of the

Ethiopians," whose eunuch was converted to Christianity (Acts 8:27-39).

Makeda is known to us as the Queen of Sheba, and her story is told in the Ethiopian text *Kebra Nagast*, or the *Glory of the Kings*, which was written around 1321 CE. She is said to have reigned around 1000 BCE.

Makeda's father was a foreigner who arrived in Ethiopia to find the people were being oppressed by a wicked snake. He killed a goat and filled its guts with poison, then left it for the snake. The snake ate it and died, and in gratitude, the people made him king.

The king had a daughter, Makeda, who succeeded him as the ruler of Sheba. Having heard of the wealth of Solomon's kingdom from Ethiopian merchants who traded with Israel, she set off to Jerusalem. She toured the sights, studied with the wise King Solomon, and even accepted Solomon's Jewish faith.

The night before she returned to Sheba, Solomon offered her a heavily spiced and salty farewell banquet. Cunningly, he provided nothing for her to drink. He then persuaded her to sleep in the same room with him, but she made him swear to take nothing from her by force. He made her swear the same oath in return.

As part of his plan, Solomon had placed a bowl of clear water in the middle of the room between their beds. Makeda became more and more thirsty, but when she tiptoed to the bowl and started to drink, Solomon woke and accused her of taking the water by force, breaking her promise.

He told her that since she had broken her word, his was no longer valid, and they slept together as Solomon had planned. In the morning, Solomon gave Makeda a ring. He told her if she bore a male child, she must send the child to Jerusalem with the ring as a token. Despite her opposition, her son, Bayna Lekhem, eventually won her permission to go to Jerusalem. Solomon loved Bayna Lekhem and wanted him to succeed the throne of the Kingdom of Israel, but the youth insisted on returning to Ethiopia. Some say that Solomon gave him the Ark of the Covenant, while others say Bayna Lekhem stole it from the temple, putting a perfect duplicate in its place. Some believe Ethiopia still holds the Ark of the Covenant, or the Tabot, in the Church of St Mary of Zion at Aksum.

Bayna Lekhem, or in Arabic, Ibn al-Hakim, "son of the wise man," became the first emperor of Ethiopia. He took the regnal name Menelik I, which is simply a translation of Ibn al-Hakim and emphasizes the descent of the Ethiopian royal house from King Solomon. Menelik was the first emperor of the Solomonic dynasty that ruled Ethiopia all the way to the time of Haile Selassie, who was deposed in 1974.

The truth is more prosaic. Historians believe the Solomonic dynasty was founded in 1262 CE when the last Zagwe ruler of Ethiopia was deposed. Yekuno Amlak took power in Amharaland (the central province of Ethiopia) as Emperor Tesfa Iyasus. And as stated above, some scholars believe the Queen of Sheba ruled in Yemen, not Ethiopia, while others believe she never existed at all.

One African king who entered European mythology but was never found in Africa was Prester John. Originally thought to be a ruler of India, by 1250, Westerners were beginning to think that he ruled over Ethiopia, either as its king or as the head of the Ethiopian Church. In 1441, Emperor Zara Yaqob of Ethiopia sent delegates to the Council of Florence, an ecumenical council of the Catholic Church. Those delegates were flabbergasted to find they were representing "Prester John." To them, he was Kwestantinos I (Zara Yaqob) of the House of Solomon. Not for the last time, Europeans were showing themselves unable to distinguish between African fact and fiction.

Some African myths about the foundation of kingdoms include references to the Muslim and Arab world. Djenne in Mali is well known for its immense mudbrick mosque and other adobe architecture. It was an important town on the Saharan trade route, like Timbuktu. One man from the country near Djenne had gone to Arabia, where he fought on behalf of the Prophet Muhammad. Muhammad noticed how bravely the man fought, and after the battle, he asked who he was and where he had come from.

The warrior told him, and Muhammad said, "Go home to your country, and you will found a great city that will become a jewel of Islam."

The man went back to Djenne, where he secured a site for his new city. But every time he tried to build the city walls, they collapsed. Eventually, he asked the Bozo and Nono tribes that lived nearby to help him. They told him there was a spirit living there who was breaking down the walls. The spirit would have to be given a sacrifice.

Some people say that the head of the Bozo tribe gave his daughter to be buried alive on the site of the city. Others say that the warrior himself had to make that sacrifice. Whichever version you accept, the story seems a rather odd mix of African traditions and Islamic history.

Yaa Asantewaa, unlike the Queen of Sheba, is a verifiable historical figure. She was the war leader of the Ashanti Kingdom in Ghana.

Yaa Asantewaa was born in 1840. Her brother, Nana Akwasi Afrane Opese, was the ruler of Edwesu, and she became queen mother of Ejisu. During her brother's reign, the British were putting pressure on the Ashanti Empire, as they were on much of the rest of Africa. At the same time, recent civil wars had weakened the Ashanti. When Yaa Asantewaa's brother died, she nominated her grandson as ruler of Edwesu and became regent for him when he, together with the king of Ashanti, was exiled by the British.

The British demanded the Golden Stool of the Ashanti, the symbol of their sovereignty and royalty. A council meeting was held to discuss what action to take. Several Ashanti nobles proposed compliance. Yaa Asantewaa disagreed; the Ashanti had been humiliated, and it was time for them to fight. She seized a gun and fired it into the air to show her willingness to lead. She was chosen to lead the Ashanti army against the British.

This was the last hurrah of the Ashanti Empire. The British drafted new troops, and Yaa Asantewaa was exiled to the Seychelles, where she died in 1921. But she is much loved and respected in Ghana as an opponent of British colonialism and a foremother of Ghanaian independence, which was won at last in 1957.

Another much-respected queen was **Queen Tin Hinane of the Tuareg.** She fled from the rich lands of the Maghreb (modern Morocco and Algeria) when she became pregnant out of wedlock. Her servant Takamata accompanied her on her flight; Takamata was also pregnant.

But in the middle of the Sahara, they exhausted their food supply. Tin Hinane was exhausted and close to death. Takamata could see no trees, no plants, and no animals, but she found an anthill and broke it open. Inside the anthill, she found the grain that the ants had stored, which she brought back to her queen. The sparse meal restored Tin Hinane's energy, and they were able to continue.

When they got to Tamanrasset, the queen gave birth to a daughter, and Takamata had twins, both girls. They were the founding mothers of the Tuareg, and the Tuareg remain a matrilineal people to this day.

Shaka Zulu was the founder of the Zulu Empire and transformed the history of the Zulu people. He was born Shaka kaSenzangakhona around 1787 and was an illegitimate son of King Senzangakhona kaJama. Shaka fought as a unit leader and later as a general under Inkosi Dingiswayo, prince and later king of the Mthethwa Empire. Dingiswayo had consolidated power by assimilating nearby chiefdoms, which influenced Shaka's policies. Even though Shaka created a huge and fearsome army, he often preferred to take power through diplomacy.

In 1816, when Shaka's father died, Shaka decided to claim the chiefdom from his half-brother Sigujana. A year later, Dingiswayo was killed in battle by Zwide of the Nxumalo. Shaka welcomed what was left of the Mthethwa army into his own fighting force and set out for revenge. He had Zwide's mother shut up in a house full of hyenas, which killed and ate her, but he was unable to get his hands on Zwide until much later.

Shaka turned the Zulu people into a nation of warriors. He changed the way they fought, introducing a shorter stabbing spear instead of the thrown assegai and teaching his men how to use their shields to knock aside the enemy's shields, leaving them unprotected. It's said that he made his men march without sandals to toughen their feet, and his army could move fast when it needed to, marching up to fifty miles a day.

Shaka also appears to have invented the famous Zulu "bull horn" formation. The "chest" or center of his army would fight close with the enemy, and then the "horns" would enter the battle, outflanking the enemy on both sides. Just in case the enemy broke out, the bull's "loins" waited in the wings, giving Shaka's men confidence that they had a fresh reserve force.

Despite his success, Shaka made some serious enemies, particularly after the death of his mother, Nandi, in 1827. He seems to have gone slightly mad with grief; he executed thousands of people, ordered that no crops should be planted, and commanded that no milk was to be drunk. When he sent most of his forces north on a campaign the next year, his half-brothers assassinated him. Dingane took the chiefdom.

Oba Oduduwa was the Olofin (traditional ruler) of Ile-Ife and the Divine King of Yoruba. In Yoruba tradition, he is said to have been the first ruler of the state of Ife and the ancestor of the royal houses of Yorubaland. Many people say that every Yoruba is descended from Oba Oduduwa.

Before Oduduwa's time, the Ife area was divided into thirteen different states, each with its own Oba (divine king). As Olofin of the city of Ile-Ife, Oduduwa used his influence to bring the thirteen states together into a single kingdom, usurping his brother Obatala and creating a dynasty that included not only the first Ooni of Ile-Ife (spiritual leader of the Yoruba people) but also the ruling houses of Benin and the Oyo Empire.

However, some Muslims prefer to believe that Oduduwa was a prince of Mecca who was exiled to Africa.

Where things become slightly confusing is that Oduduwa and his brother Obatala are seen by the Yoruba as not just historical figures but also primordial gods or orishas. They were as old as time and sent by the creator Olodumare. So, whether they belong to the realm of myth or the real world or both is an intriguing question.

The same questions can be asked about the story of **Sunjata (Sundiata) Keita**, who founded the Mali Empire. The Sunjata epic has been sung by griots for centuries, and we know that Sunjata did exist since Arab traveler-historians ibn Battuta and ibn Khaldun both corroborate certain elements of his story. However, historians have suspected some of the details might have been added later.

According to the epic, two wives, the beautiful Sassouma Bereté and the ugly hunchback Sogolon Condé, of Chief Nare Famagan became pregnant at the same time. Sogolon gave birth to Sunjata and sent an old woman from her hut to tell her husband that her long-awaited heir had arrived. However, the old woman stopped to eat on the way to the king's hut, so the news of Sunjata's half-brother's birth arrived first. Dankaran Touman, Sunjata's half-brother, was accepted as the firstborn and made Nare Famagan's heir.

Sassouma Bereté suspected Sogolon Condé meant her no good, so she had spells cast to cripple Sunjata. The boy had to crawl on his hands and feet, and his mother was humiliated. When she asked Sassouma Bereté to give her some baobab leaves for a special meal, her rival told her nastily to ask Sunjata to climb a tree and pick them.

"Why can't you get up?" Sogolon Condé asked her son angrily.

"I will," he said and asked the blacksmiths to forge iron bars for him to use as crutches. However, when he tried to get up, he snapped them. He then asked for a stick made of the wood of the jonba tree, which his mother cut for him. Using this, Sunjata was able to get up and walk.

As he walked, he became stronger, and he made his way toward the baobab tree. By the time he got to it, he had become extremely strong.

So, instead of picking the leaves, he picked up the entire tree and carried it back to his mother's compound.

Dankaran Touman eventually became king. Sunjata became a great hunter, but he never challenged his half-brother for the throne. However, Dankaran Touman still felt threatened, so he asked the nine witches of the Manden region to get rid of his rival. In return for this favor, Dankaran Touman gave them an ox to share between them. When Sunjata found this out, he gave the witches nine buffalo—one each—and they promised never to interfere with Sunjata.

Then, seeing he could never live with his brother, Sunjata went into exile to Mema, together with his mother and younger siblings.

Dankaran Touman was a weak ruler, and his realm was eventually invaded by Sumanguru, who took over the country and ruled as a tyrant. No one knew where Sunjata had gone, so a mission was sent out with spices from Manden country. In every town and village, they laid out their spices in the market. No one knew what they were. Then, in Mema, Sunjata's sister saw the spices and quickly bought them all, inviting the traders to come and eat with her. Sunjata was there, of course, and the members of the mission asked him to reconquer the Manden. Sunjata said his mother was too old to travel, and he had to stay with her. When his mother died quietly that night, he knew that he was fated to rule the Manden's thirty-three clans.

Sunjata invaded, but he couldn't defeat Sumanguru, who was defended by potent magic. Sunjata's sister, Sogolon Kulunkan, who was a great beauty, set out for Sumanguru's palace to seduce him. Sumanguru wanted to sleep with her, but she would not enter the bedchamber until he told her all his secrets.

Sumanguru's mother was passing by the tent and warned him, "Don't tell your secrets to a one-night stand!" Of course, this advice made Sumanguru mad, and he did exactly the opposite. He told Sogolon Kulunkan that the only thing that could kill him was an arrow tipped with a white cock's spur. Sogolon Kulunkan agreed to come into the bedchamber but said she needed to wash first. She took a long time. Sumanguru called her, and she answered, "Wait a bit!" He waited and called again. Again, she told him to wait. He got fed up with waiting and went to the privy and found she had run away, leaving two magical amulets to speak on her behalf and give her time to escape.

Now, Sunjata had the secret. He made a cock-spur-tipped arrow and set out to find Sumanguru during the next battle. Sumanguru fled, making his horse leap the wide Niger River, but Sunjata's arrow struck him just as he reached the other side.

After Sunjata had established his empire, he wanted horses. He sent to the king of Jolof to buy some. But the king refused to sell, instead sending scraps of leather with the insulting message, "He's a hunter, not a king. Let him make shoes. He can walk wherever he needs to go." Sunjata declared war on the Jolof Empire and made Tira Magan Traore his general. Every time Tira Magan won a battle, he said, "I serve a hunter; I'm only walking the dogs." Finally, he caught the king of Jolof and cut off his head, saying, "The dogs had a good walk. I'm going home."

Sunjata died in 1255 and was succeeded in turn by three of his sons. Eventually, his brother's side of the family took over the succession, and in 1312, the great-nephew of Sunjata, Mansa Musa, acceded to the throne.

Mansa Musa is often referred to as the world's richest man. By the time he inherited the empire, Mali had become immensely wealthy. It controlled the salt trade from the north through the Sahara and the gold trade from southern Africa. The whole area of the Niger Delta contained at least four hundred cities with a high standard of living. The Mali Empire had become a true urban civilization.

Musa incorporated the cities of Gao and Timbuktu into the Mali Empire, greatly increasing its size. He also extended friendly ties with the Muslim sultanates of the north and made Timbuktu a center of Muslim scholarship, creating the University of Sankore. Musa's worldview was highly cosmopolitan, and he attracted scholars and artists from all over the Muslim world. In addition, he sponsored building projects, including mosques and madrasas.

In 1324, Musa went on hajj to Mecca, taking a huge entourage (some sources say that sixty thousand servants accompanied him) and vast supplies of gold with him. In Cairo, his liberal handing out of gifts caused hyperinflation. He ensured Mali made a reputation abroad as a wealthy and civilized country, and this reputation traveled as far as the West. In the Catalan Atlas, produced around 1375, Mansa Musa is shown with a golden crown and orb, sitting in state in the middle of the map of Africa.

Ras Tafari was the last emperor of Ethiopia, and although his life spans the 19th and 20th centuries, he, too, blurs the lines between history and myth.

He was born Lij Tafari Makonnen and baptized as Haile Selassie. He is called Ras Tafari from the noble title "Ras" added to his secular name. Born in 1892, he was the son of Makonnen Wolde Mikael, the governor of Harar. He became influential in the court of Empress Zewditu and appears to have been involved in some form of coup against Lij Iyasu, the original heir to the throne who was rumored to have converted to Islam.

Zewditu made Ras Tafari crown prince in 1916, and he appears to have acted effectively as her prime minister. When she died in 1930, he became Negusa Nagast, "king of kings," of Ethiopia. Although he was not of the direct line, he had Solomonic lineage through his grandmother, which allowed him to take the throne.

As Emperor Haile Selassie, he embarked on the cautious modernization of what was still, at that point, a feudal state. He was responsible for Ethiopia's admission to the League of Nations, the predecessor of the United Nations, and he became a celebrity on his tours of Europe, Egypt, and the Middle East. In Jerusalem, he adopted forty Armenian orphans who had lost their parents in the Armenian genocide; they were taught music in Addis Ababa and became the imperial brass band. He also was instrumental in forming the Organisation of African Unity in 1963, the precursor of today's African Union.

Reforming Ethiopia was difficult. Haile Selassie gave the country a constitution, but it did not deliver full democracy due to the objections of the nobles. Even his tax reforms had to be diluted. The invasion of Ethiopia by the Italians in the 1930s forced him into exile in Britain, and when he liberated the country, it was with the help of the British Army. Unfortunately, he faced a dilemma; any reform was too much for the nobles but not enough for the younger generation.

In the early 1970s, Haile Selassie faced major problems. Eritrea had been included in Ethiopia after the Second World War, but it was fighting a war for independence, which it eventually won in 1991. This conflict stretched the country's resources. At the same time, there were famines in the northern areas: Wollo and Tigray. In 1974, Haile Selassie was deposed and imprisoned, and he died in 1975 under suspicious circumstances.

So far, you have been reading about the historical head of an African state. However, for a large number of people around the world, he is much more. The Rastafarian movement began in the 1930s in Jamaica as an offshoot of Marcus Garvey's pan-Africanist group. According to Rastafarians, Ras Tafari was the Messiah who would lead the African diaspora to freedom; in other words, he was God incarnate.

Haile Selassie visited Jamaica in 1966, where he was greeted by over 100,000 Rastafarians at the airport in Kingston. He never explicitly denied their belief in him as God and granted some Rastafarians land to live on in Ethiopia.

* * *

Right now, we're seeing the creation of new mythical "versions" of African rulers. For instance, Netflix has courted controversy by casting a Black actor as Cleopatra VII Philopator (*that* Cleopatra). She was descended from a Macedonian family and was probably, if not white, only mildly brown-skinned. Arguably, this matters more to us now than it did to Egyptians in Cleopatra's day, who were a remarkably cosmopolitan bunch and had already been ruled by Libyans, Persians, and Nubians.

African rulers figure in many video games and TV shows. Shaka Zulu features in *Civilization*, the Queen of Sheba appears as Bilquis in Neil Gaiman's *American Gods*, and Yaa Asantewaa has had a British radio series and a Ghanaian TV documentary dedicated to her. Mansa Musa appears in *Civilization* and faces off against Jeff Bezos in the YouTube series "Epic Rap Battles of History." (It's well worth watching!) Meanwhile, the Marvel universe includes the country Wakanda, which draws on African mythology and is represented as an African technological hub and superpower.

And, of course, modern African rulers are continuing to make history. Nelson Mandela achieved legendary status with his successful life-long campaign against apartheid and his term as the first-ever president of the "Rainbow Nation." Ellen Johnson Sirleaf became the first woman as an elected head of state in Africa when she became the twenty-fourth president of Liberia (2006–2016). Perhaps in the 22nd century, kids will be watching Mandela the superhero battling the forces of evil on their mobile phones.

Chapter 9: Shamanic Stories

Shamanism is a tradition in which practitioners use trance or drugs to achieve an altered state of consciousness and communicate with spirit beings. For instance, Siberian and Arctic shamans use drumming to create a trance state in which they can talk to animal spirits, such as the bear.

Possession allows people to communicate with the realm of gods and spirits (including, as always, ancestors) and is common in most African religious traditions, including those that have spread to the Americas and the Caribbean. However, it's not always called "shamanism." Masked dances, for instance, are a common way for individuals to communicate with gods or their ancestors, and in many African cultures, divination is the most important aspect of spiritual communication.

For instance, illness is seen as often being due to witchcraft or to magical or religious reasons, such as failing to observe rituals or taboos. This doesn't rule out scientific explanations; instead, it complements them. Someone may have a heart attack because he has a weak heart but also because a work colleague wished ill on him. Divination is used by healers to find the causes of illnesses or problems such as infertility, and then a second divination is often carried out to ascertain the right treatment.

In the Kongo religion, a nganga (plural banganga) can communicate with spirits and ancestors. The job of the nganga is to divine the causes of any illness and to heal. They often wear frightening costumes. Some wear white masks (white is the color of the dead), while others wear thick white eyeshadow and red and yellow stripes on their faces. They sometimes dress in wild animal skins and wear necklaces of animal teeth.

Banganga, like other shamans, are both religious and medical at the same time—a duality recognized in the pejorative name "witch doctor." In fact, Christian priests in Kongo areas were often referred to as banganga; like the shamans, they were seen as go-betweens, taking messages between the human and spiritual worlds.

While the Siberian shamans made their own drums as part of their initiation, the banganga would create a nkisi sculpture and charge it with spiritual power. A medicine pack would be placed in a hollow inside the nkisi, similar to the way in which Native American medicine men create their own medicine bag as a source of power and healing. The nkisi then had to be activated by driving nails or blades into it and by chanting.

In South Africa, two kinds of practitioners are found. There are inyanga, who are similar to the banganga, and sangomas, traditional healers. Their domains are different but not mutually exclusive.

Sangomas always have a "calling," sometimes in a dream or a vision. (This, again, is a common feature of almost all shamanic traditions.) If the person who has been called ignores their calling, they will find bad luck following them. They might experience severe illness until they accept the calling and seek out a teacher. The apprenticeship period involves living with a teacher, often in austere conditions and in relative isolation, for a period that can stretch from several months to years.

The training ends with a sacrifice and the final test of finding things that have been hidden. The other sangomas will hide the skin and gall bladder of a goat that has been sacrificed, as well as the apprentice's sacred divinatory bones. The apprentice sangoma has to find where they are.

Sangomas make their divination by throwing the bones. All illness is a form of disharmony, so the sangoma's task is to find out what will bring back balance, harmony, and health. That might be within an individual or within a family or community. The sangoma may then throw the bones again for specific advice, which can include reconciliation with estranged relatives, herbal medicines, or even Western medicine.

Muthi, or herbal medicines, which are usually psychoactive drugs, are often added to bathing water or steamed for inhalation. Some may be used as enemas or as emetics (to induce vomiting). Most sangomas collect their own herbs in accordance with advice from ancestors on the right time and right place to find them. Again, divination may be used as a way of finding where to get the herbs, or an ancestor may speak directly to the sangoma.

Every sangoma is possessed by ancestor spirits. But many now have to divide their lives between being a traditional sangoma and living a modern life, working in a university or in modern healthcare. There is a growing LGBTQ+ sangoma movement too, showing how the tradition is gradually evolving to accept different lifestyles. (In fact, a female sangoma can be possessed by the spirit of a male ancestor and the other way around, so despite the gender-inflexible nature of traditional Zulu society, this is not as big of a stretch as it may seem.)

There are even some white sangomas now. This has ruffled feathers among some, but other traditional healers explain that even though a white sangoma may have no African ancestors, they may be called on by "foreign spirits" that their ancestors had a significant relationship with. For instance, someone whose great-grandfather killed a Zulu may be called by that spirit.

Credo Mutwa, a Zulu shaman, traveled the path from indigenous traditional healer to New Age guru. He got involved with extraterrestrial encounters and ufologists. He also adapted elements of the Dogon creation myth. While for some, he gave a seal of authenticity to anything he touched as a traditionally trained sangoma, for others, he was simply a fraud and an opportunist or an oddball. He created what he called African cultural villages; seen as tourist traps at one time, people are now coming around to the view of Mutwa as an outsider artist, and the villages are being interpreted as art installations rather than museum-like institutions.

Zimbabwe has Shona spirit mediums who are similar to the sangomas. They are the svikiro and, like the sangomas, undergo possession by ancestral spirits who can give them advice. By helping keep balance and mediating between the spiritual and human worlds, the svikiro protect their society. Thus, they are given high status and respect. They are also often (though not always) healers.

Some of the spirits they channel are mhondoro, "lions," which are the spirits of kings and chieftains. It's interesting that while there's a perception that many traditional practices are dying out, after the civil war in Zimbabwe, there was a huge revival in spirit medium practices. People were looking for help with their experiences of violence, and the svikiro gave them a way of processing and dealing with their trauma.

Possession by gods and spirits is common in African ceremonies. It is often brought about by drumming, dancing, or both. The spirit possessing the person may make particular demands for food, drink, or clothing or may perform certain repetitive acts. The person possessed may not remember anything they have done while in a trance.

Ancestor worship and veneration are the basis of the majority of African cultures, and shamanic possession gives people a way to channel communications to and from their ancestors. It is also a potent way of unifying a group of people, such as a particular age group or a secret society.

The trance element is particularly important in African-origin religions that grew up in the New World, such as Candomblé and Voodoo (Vodou). In Brazilian Candomblé, for instance, a woman may dress up as Oshun (Oxúm) in yellow, holding the sacred fan in one hand, and dance Oshun's dance until she feels the imminent presence of the goddess. If someone in the congregation is possessed, the other members of the terreiro (temple) can communicate directly with the goddess through her (or sometimes him).

Divination is also common in many African societies and is usually performed by a practitioner who could be identified as a shaman. There are a number of stories about how divination was discovered. In Yoruba lore, the goddess Oshun wears a necklace of cowrie shells, symbolizing the sixteen shells that are used for Erindinlogun divination. She got them from her husband Orunmila, the god of divination. Other gods, like Eshu, use kola nuts. Whether cowries or nuts, the items are thrown on a cloth or a divination board, and the position in which they fall is then interpreted by the diviner.

Divination is so central to African thought that it is even used in worship, such as to determine whether a sacrifice has been acceptable to a god.

Not all shamans are good ones. A lot of today's sangomas are fed up with seeing classified ads in newspapers or on the internet for fake sangomas and mediums. Some sangoma trainers abuse their apprentices or use them as unpaid servants. Other sangomas make their clients dependent on them and demand more and more money and gifts from them while giving little in return.

Mali has a salutary tale of a shaman who ran a protection racket. He protected the cattle of one village from a ferocious lion; in return, he expected a nice fat cow to be given to him from time to time.

When a huntsman shot a huge lion nearby, the villagers breathed a sigh of relief. They thought they would no longer need to pay the shaman. Just as a precaution, they moved their herds to the other side of the river since a shaman can't cross running water. However, the shaman turned up, furious that he hadn't been paid, and found a ferryman to take him across. The villagers noticed the shaman's golden eyes, pointy teeth, and flowing mane of long hair. Suddenly, the shaman turned into a lion and sprang onto the fattest cow in the herd and ate her all up.

Fortunately, the ferryman was actually a local river god who decided the lion was fair game. He had a magic bow and arrow with him. The villagers never had any more problems with lions eating their cows.

Conclusion

African mythology infuses African cultures. While there are many different strands of African myth, you have probably noticed that many myths reflect similar concerns or have similar situations. Eshu and Legba are not by any means the same, but they are similar gods with similar positions in the pantheon. Many myths stress the enmity of half-brothers in a polygamous household against the solidarity of mothers and sisters.

But African myths aren't just for Africans. Many of the stories moved to the New World with African slaves and now make up a major part of Black American cultures. Anansi became Aunt Nancy in Jamaica, while the Yoruba and Fon pantheons were imported wholesale into Voodoo, Vodoun, Vodou, and Santeria. In the US, the trickster hare became Br'er Rabbit, who, through books and then through the Disney film *Song of the South* in 1949, became part of mainstream American culture.

It's interesting that African myths retain their fluidity on the other side of the Atlantic. For instance, in the Afro-Cuban religion, gods remain polysemous with multiple personalities. This is referred to as one *oricha* having several *caminos* or different paths. Sometimes, gods from different African traditions are blended together. Most of the American African-origin religions have blended to some extent with Catholicism. For instance, Oshun is often identified with the Virgin Mary and Ogum with Saint Anthony of Padua. (Some practitioners are now trying to "purify" or "re-Africanize" the religion by taking out the Catholic references.)

Most African traditional graphic and sculptural art relates to mythology. There are figures of gods and spirits, power fetishes, and ritual paraphernalia, such as the divination board. African art, having been dismissed during the 19th century as "primitive" and not worth preserving, was discovered by a generation of artists that included Picasso; it showed them new ways of seeing things. Appreciating how these artworks fit into the mythological and ritual pattern, though, stops us from simply appropriating them; we can see them in their context rather than just as "fine art."

And today, there's a whole lot of creative work going on that uses African myths, gods, and stories as a background. For instance, in contemporary science fiction and fantasy, Neil Gaiman's *American Gods* features Mr. Nancy, a tailor, drawing on Anansi's story. Other African gods also appear, including Mr. Ibis (the Egyptian god Thoth) and the goddess Yemoja.

Increasingly, people of color are writing fantasy and science fiction and using their own backgrounds as part of the setting. For instance, Paris-based Aliette de Bodard uses Vietnamese culture in her intricate space operas. African settings and stories have come to fantasy through such writers as Nigerian-American Nnedi Okorafor, whose characters include an albino witch, Legba, and a trickster spider. She espouses "Africanfuturism." Jordan Ifueko is another Nigerian-American speculative fiction writer. Her book *Raybearer* created a future world that is definitely African in background, though it is not in any way a pastiche of Yoruba myths.

Comics and now TV have accepted Africa as a full partner in their worlds. A breakthrough in this regard was the films *Black Panther* (2018) and *Wakanda Forever* (2022), which feature a black superhero and strong, authentic elements of African costume, such as the Zulu isicholo hat worn by the Queen Mother Ramonda. The films have gained a much greater audience than the comics and have even inspired African leaders in business and government to think about creating Wakanda-like technological cities.

For the last few hundred years, Greek and Roman mythology held pride of place. Look at the classical portico of the White House, and you can see how much the Greek ideal resonated with Americans at the time. Maybe in the next few hundred years, we'll see a lot more African mythology and influences across the world.

Here's another book by Enthralling History that you might like

Free limited time bonus

Stop for a moment. We have a free bonus set up for you. The problem is this: we forget 90% of everything that we read after 7 days. Crazy fact, right? Here's the solution: we've created a printable, 1-page pdf summary for this book that you're reading now. All you have to do to get your free pdf summary is to go to the following website:

https://livetolearn.lpages.co/enthrallinghistory/

Once you do, it will be intuitive. Enjoy, and thank you!

Bibliography

Barker, William H. West African Folk-Tales. CMS Bookshop, Lagos, 1917.

Barnes, Sandra T & Ben-Amos, Paula. "Benin, Oyo, and Dahomey: Warfare, State Building, and the Sacralization of Iron in West African History." *Expedition Magazine* 25.2 (1983). Penn Museum, 1983.

Burstein, Stanley, ed. Ancient African Civilizations: Kush and Axum. Princeton, N.J., 1998.

Chidester, David. Credo Mutwa, Zulu Shaman: The Invention and Appropriation of Indigenous Authenticity in African Folk Religion. Journal for the Study of Religion, Vol 15, No 2 (2002) pp/ 65-85.

Diop, Cheikh Anta. The African Origin of Civilization: Myth or Reality. New York, 1974.

Diop, Ismahan Soukeyna. African Mythology, Femininity, and Maternity. Springer Nature Switzerland. Cham, 2019.

Griaule, Marcel. Conversations with Ogotemmeli: An Introduction to Dogon Religious Ideas. Oxford University Press, Oxford. 1965.

Jonker, Ingrid. A study of how a sangoma makes sense of her 'sangomahood' through narrative. University of Pretoria, MA dissertation, 2006.

LaGamma, Alisa. Art and Oracle: African Art and Rituals of Divination. Metropolitan Museum of Art, New York, 2000.

Lugira, Aloysius M. African Traditional Religion. Chelsea House, New York. 2009.

Murphy, Joseph M and Sandford, Mei-Mei. Osun Across the Waters: A Yoruba Goddess in Africa and the Americas. Indiana University Press, Bloomington Indiana, 2001.

Nkabinde, Nkunzi Zandile. Black Bull, Ancestors and Me: My Life as a Lesbian Sangoma. Fanele, Auckland Park SA. 2008.

Ogundipe, Ayodele. Eshu Elegbara: Chance, Uncertainly in Yoruba Mythology. Kwara State University Press, Ilorin, 2012.

Peek, Philip M and Yankah, Kwesi. African Folklore: An Encyclopedia. Routledge, New York and London, Shakarov, Avner, and Senatorova, Lyubov. Traditional African Art: An Illustrated Study. McFarland & Company, Jefferson NC. 2015.

Skertchly, J. A. Dahomey As It Is: Being A Narrative of Eight Months' Residence in That Country, With a Full Account of the Notorious Annual Customs. Chapman & Hall, London, 1874.

Passé, Présent et Futur des Palais et Sites Royaux d'Abomey. Getty Conservation Institute, Los Angeles. 1999.

Wallis Budge, Ernest Alfred. Legends of the Gods. London, 1912.

Žabkar, Louis V. Hymns to Isis in Her Temple at Philae. Brandeis University Press. 1988.